Mount Laurel Library
Mount Laurel, NJ 08054
Phone 234-7319

DEMCO

City of Silence

⊂ℨ

City of Silence

LISTENING TO HIROSHIMA

— ⚬ —

Rachelle Linner

ORBIS BOOKS

Maryknoll, New York 10545

The Catholic Foreign Mission Society of America (Maryknoll) recruits and trains people for overseas missionary service. Through Orbis Books, Maryknoll aims to foster the international dialogue that is essential to mission. The books published, however, reflect the opinions of their authors and are not meant to represent the official position of the society.

Manufactured in the United States of America

Library of Congress Cataloging-in-Publication Data

Linner, Rachelle.
 City of silence: listening to Hiroshima / by Rachelle Linner.
  p. cm.
 ISBN 1-57075-014-9
 1. Hiroshima-shi (Japan)—History—Bombardment, 1945. 2. Nagasaki -shi (Japan)—History—Bombardment, 1945. 3. Atomic bomb victims— Japan. 4. Atomic bomb victims—United States. I. Title.
 D767.25.H6L46 1995
 952'.195404—dc20   94-45689
                                                          CIP

To

JAMES F. MORGAN, S.J.

with gratitude for the witness

of his life of dedicated service

Contents

— ☙ —

Acknowledgments

——— C3 ———

I have both a photo album and a scrapbook from my trip to Japan. In the scrapbook are the name cards of the people I met, pages from my calendar with notations of interviews, ticket stubs (from a baseball game, museums, an aquarium, and a performance of traditional Japanese dance), articles about me that had appeared in a Hiroshima newspaper, and photographs given to me by hibakusha (photos of trees in the Peace Park that had grown beyond the visible scars of radiation damage; one from August 6, 1945, of hibakusha gathering in front of a police station). In my enthusiasm I was certain that I would never forget the people I met in Hiroshima — but of course I have, and it saddens me that each time I look at the scrapbook it is harder and harder to remember the faces that go with the names. My enthusiastic certainty that I would foster friendships with several people foundered on the sober reality of language barriers, and I find that each year I exchange fewer and fewer New Year's greetings with Japanese acquaintances.

Yet it was a happy task to compile these acknowledgments to the many and generous people I met on my Hiroshima sojourn. Their gifts of word and story became the threads that allowed me to weave the tapestry of images that this book is. I am, of course, responsible for any errors in the way I have shaded or placed their words in the composition, and I am not so naive as to believe that they would all agree with my presentation.

I apologize in advance if I have inadvertently omitted the names of people who belong on this list. Also omitted, although I hope it can be discerned in the way I talk of their books, are the thanks I owe to the authors who educated and inspired me about this massive subject. When I reflect on that diverse group of authors and scholars I am, once again, awed by the privilege of literacy.

For practical reasons I have divided this list into hibakusha, interpreters, and those who provided specific assistance on this book. I use the term "interpreter" broadly, and it includes both the people who generously translated Japanese into English and those who shared their insight, passion, and sensitivity about Hiroshima through their activism, scholarship, journalism, photography, fiction, and poetry.

I thank these people for their help, but I also thank them for welcoming me into their community of concern. Some of these people met me only in the early days of my ignorance, but others walked with me over the years, as my interest deepened and my understanding of these issues became more subtle and sophisticated. I look back to the first years after my trip with mingled embarrassment and affection for my innocent enthusiasm, and I am all the more grateful that these good teachers saw beyond my naivete and bestowed on me the inestimable compliment of taking my commitment seriously. I hope I might some day have the opportunity to repay that favor by providing that same quality of respectful attention to another novice.

Hibakusha: Susumu Ishitani, Ichiro Kawamoto, Koshiro Kondo, Hirotu Kubouro, Kanji Kuramoto, Kiyoshi Kuramoto, M.D., Sadako Kurihara, Miyoko Matsubara, Yoshito Matsushige, Hiromu Morishita, Ichiro Moritaki, Rev. Motoi Munakata, Suzuko Numata, Keiko Ogura, Miyao Ohara, Sil Gun Ri, Tazu Shibama, Kiyoshi Shimizu, M.D., Chiyo Takeuchi, Kiyoshi Tanimoto, Setsuko Thurlow, Michiko Yamaoka.

Interpreters: Tadatoshi Akiba, Mizuhoko Kotani Asanuma, Robert Del Tredici, Setsumi Del Tredici, Keiko Doi, Eileen Egan, Tomin Harada, M.D., Doris Hartman, Walter Hooke, Kyoko Ishikure, Chikako Ito, M.D., Kaori Kuramajii, Rhiana Levy, Junko Maeda, Richard McSorley, S.J., Naoko Naganuma, Tomoko Nakamura, Yoko Ninomiya, Kaoru Ogura, Minoru Ohmuta, Hajime Okita, M.D., Michiko Okita, M.D., Barbara Reynolds, Shoko Shintani, Rinjiro Sodei, Dorothy Stroup, Fumiko Susakida, Charles Sutton, Helen Sutton, David L. Swain, Akira Tashiro, Michiko Tashiro, Helen Redding Wiegel, Kaori Yagishita, Michiko Yamane, Yukio Yokohara.

Book Assistance: I am grateful to those who read all or part of this manuscript. In an early version, the chapter on American hibakusha was read by Jenny Morizumi, Dorothy Stroup, and David L. Swain. The chapter on Barbara Reynolds was read by L. Joan Brown. The manuscript in its entirety was read by Robert Ellsberg, Laura Sapelly, David L. Swain, and Kassie Temple. I asked them to be attentive to factual errors or unfounded suppositions, and their suggestions and comments have made this a stronger book. I am responsible for whatever errors of fact or interpretation remain. I am indebted to Randie Margolis, Ph.D., for the conversations that helped me to elucidate the universal themes embedded in Hiroshima's story.

If it is true that our work is revealed to us by the community to which we belong, then I am particularly grateful to Robert Ellsberg. He generously called me a writer — a name I had been too timid to give to myself — and then used his considerable gifts as an editor to hone my writing to a deeper authority and maturity. Although at times I rewrote with less than good cheer I never regretted my decision to trust his judgment rather than my own.

Many years ago Jim Douglass and I were talking about a mutual acquaintance, a writer, and I found myself excusing his rudeness by praising his talent. Jim reminded me that "talent is not a virtue," and although I regularly forget the truth of that statement, I just as regularly recall it, each time with renewed delight for the perspective it offers. When I would feel disheartened during the times that writing was slow and laborious, I would be consoled by the thought that my lack of talent would allow the readers of this book to exercise the virtue of charity. Your charity will transform the solitary act of writing into the communal gift it is meant to be, and I thank you.

Finally, because he has been, for me, a man who exemplifies the virtues of charity and humility in a particularly compelling and heroic way, I dedicate this book to Father James F. Morgan, S.J. In many ways he is responsible for whatever strengths it has. It was the luminous witness of his humility that helped me to lessen some of the tenacious self-absorption that had hampered not only my writing but my service and prayer. His example inspired me to pay attention to hibakusha, not to myself, and in the process I became a more suitable communicator of their message. In thanking him I wish to honor his life of dedicated service.

Introduction

―――― ♋ ――――

In 1984 I had the opportunity to spend six weeks in Japan, a month of that time in Hiroshima, interviewing hibakusha, the survivors of the atomic bomb explosion. The word hibakusha, which translates to "explosion-affected persons," refers both to those who were killed by and those who survived the atomic bombings. (The word is pronounced in three syllables: *hi* [as in "he"] *baku* [as in "Bach"] and *sha* [as in the "shah" of Iran.])

I first met hibakusha in 1973 when a group of Japanese peace activists visited the Washington, D.C., Community for Creative Nonviolence (CCNV), where I lived from 1971 to 1978. The hibakusha were members of a larger delegation on their way to New York to lobby at the United Nations for the abolition of nuclear weapons. In addition to making presentations to formal international organizations, the Japanese activists wanted to make connections with small, grassroots peace groups like CCNV. The large Japanese peace organizations are characterized by ideological rigidity and a penchant for intra-organizational disputes, but even had I been aware of those qualities, I doubt it would have diminished the admiration and respect for hibakusha that was engendered in me when I listened to their stories of August 6 and 9, 1945, stories they narrated with a dignified simplicity of detail and an affecting passion that was reminiscent of haiku poetry.

When I was in Japan I was repeatedly told about "the spirit of Hiroshima," the attitude that "it is war we hate, not Americans." I did not recall hearing that phrase in 1973, but that spirit was powerfully communicated by their presence among us. I sensed, but did not fully understand, that as a consequence of that moment of destruction some hibakusha had journeyed from rage through despair to a courageous and willed hope, an optimism expressed by coming to the nation that had precipitated their pain to warn us of the consequences of atomic warfare. Hibakusha desire peace with a passion fueled by their experiences of war, and it is to people like myself, who have known in contrast an almost obscene physical safety, that they have sought to convey their passion. From the ashes of their cities hibakusha have created a work of witness to

1

form a new spirit of human community, work undertaken with a dedication akin to a religious vocation. I have always felt privileged to watch and learn from this witness.

That night in 1973 I could not imagine the overwhelming destruction that had, in one moment of time, ripped their lives from the moorings of normalcy and ushered in a frenzy of grotesque injuries, burns, and the deadly, pernicious effects of radiation. After twenty years of extensive reading and careful listening to hibakusha narratives I suspect mine is still only a nascent empathy.

I have always been cognizant of my limitations, for I am a Western woman who is observing and trying to understand an event that occurred to, and has been interpreted by, Japanese men and women. Although there are times when I have spoken about hibakusha with certainty I hope I have tempered my judgments with a measure of cultural humility. My reflection and writing have also been biased by my desire to find some way to affirm their vision, honor their patient service, and praise their courage.

Fifty years after its malignant cargo was dropped over the skies of Hiroshima, we remain under the shadow of the *Enola Gay*. Hibakusha have shouldered the greatest burdens of the nuclear age, but each of us has paid a price. Some people have paid that price in a pervasive, diffuse fear engendered by nuclear weapons[1] and some people — workers at nuclear power plants and atomic veterans, among others — have known in their own and their children's bodies the damage that radiation can cause.

With the end of the Cold War and the loss of an external enemy people began to see the domestic cost of fifty years of a nuclear policy that meandered from a promised return to an Eden-like security (the same myth that informs "star wars") to "mutually assured destruction" and an eventual recognition of the need for disarmament. In some ways there is more danger now than there was at the height of the Cold War because of the widespread proliferation of nuclear weapons and the availability of weapons-grade plutonium as a by-product of nuclear power plants. There is grave concern about the safety of the arsenals of the former Soviet Union. It is possible that the 1994 confrontation between North Korea and the United States over international inspection may be the type of conflict endemic to this next phase of the nuclear age.

The demand for secrecy in the name of "national security" led to an erosion of civil liberties and the violation of trust implicit in the secret radiation tests that were conducted in the 1950s. The mishandling of radioactive waste has destroyed the environmental and human health of entire communities, whose residents consider themselves victims of "economic racism."[2] The urgency of these issues and the complex history of the past fifty years can eclipse the anniversary of the atomic bombings of Hiroshima and Nagasaki.

It is hard to remember even in Hiroshima and Nagasaki, where, long ago, hibakusha became demographic minorities. (Eighty percent of Hiroshima's present population was born after 1945.) Hibakusha are aging and each year fewer and fewer people attend the cities' annual commemoration services. The combined effect of prosperity and an educational system that ignores or sanitizes the war has resulted in large segments of the Japanese public that know or care little about hibakusha. With the gradual easing of the nuclear threat the voices of the peace movement that used to cry "No more Hiroshimas, No more Nagasakis" are softened, lulled by a sense of satisfaction that, in fact, there have been "No more hibakusha." The passage of time, the dying of hibakusha, and the ignorance of history have meant that Hiroshima and Nagasaki are seen as events of the past with little consequence for the present.

The Baal Shem Tov, the founder of Hasidism, taught that "in remembrance lies redemption," and I think of his words when I recall a woman who was exposed to the bomb as a fetus. She was born in February 1946 and diagnosed with profound mental and physical retardation. Now forty-nine years old, she requires constant care, and because she is incapable of communication or remembrance it is incumbent on us to remember for her.

Her silence marks her a true daughter of the nuclear age, because it is silence that has been at the heart of the bomb since its inception in the laboratories at the University of Chicago, Los Alamos, Oak Ridge, and Hanford. Initial press reports about Hiroshima and Nagasaki focused only on the awesome power of the bomb and omitted any mention about the effects of radiation exposure, ignorance that allowed military planners to develop the more powerful hydrogen weapons. Atomic veterans, employees at nuclear weapons plants, uranium miners, and "downwinders" (people who lived downwind from atmospheric nuclear test sites) worked for years to gain compensation for the effects of their radiation exposure. Their stories are finally being told after many years of being ignored by the press and regulatory agencies, stories that convey a sense of having been used as guinea pigs by a government that violated the mandate to protect its citizens.

Hibakusha also believe that they were guinea pigs of a scientific and political experiment, but their speech was more severely restricted by the rigid censorship that was imposed on all Japanese writing and medical studies about the bomb. That artificial seven-year silence was finally lifted in 1952, when the Allied Occupation ended, and only then were hibakusha able to measure and articulate the full dimensions of the human costs of the atomic bomb.

There are many permutations to the silence of Hiroshima, but perhaps the most frustrating is the apathy of a world enamored by weapons of mass destruction. Hibakusha's heroic, eloquent speech has been received, not with respectful listening, but with new weapons systems and bellicose posturing that make a mockery of their work for peace. That hibakusha have persisted in their work of witness is all the more remarkable in face of this humiliating rejection.

I think that many people go to Hiroshima, as I did, because of a quiet but persistent sense of despair about nuclear weapons, a faintly articulated fear that these unimaginable weapons might be used again. I went to Hiroshima as one would go on pilgrimage, to seek understanding and to see with my own eyes the place that symbolized my personal and generational history. Ironically, instead of affirming my pessimism I discovered a sense of resiliency and hope in those streets that first knew atomic death.

In retrospect, I think I was wrong to call myself a nuclear pilgrim, for if that was a true appellation I would have wanted to journey, also, to Los Alamos and the laboratories that fed it knowledge, or to the dozens of places whose names have been touched by nuclear suffering in these past fifty years. I did study the military, diplomatic, and scientific history surrounding those first atomic weapons and learned the story of the nuclear age through its impact on scientists and soldiers and the individuals and organizations who, often at great personal risk, opposed those weapons. I was a dutiful student, but as I continued my writing and research I was startled to realize that I had very little interest in the bomb or in the debates and issues of the nuclear age.

In contrast to a felt obligation to read about Robert Oppenheimer or Linus Pauling I had a deep and abiding passion to learn about Hiroshima and Nagasaki. Once I had gained a basic understanding of the facts and issues related to the atomic bomb I was eager to hear its hidden stories. I read many hibakusha narratives, the imagery of which is so vivid that there are times (especially in the summer, when Boston's heat and humidity is reminiscent of a Hiroshima August) when I will recall a particularly poignant fact with piercing detail. Inevitably (as happens with such consuming interests) I found myself meeting people like the ex-Marine who had been in Nagasaki during the Occupation; the physician who had served on Hiroshima's Atomic Bomb Casualty Commission; and the woman who, as a child, had been imprisoned by the Japanese and who forgave her captors after listening to a speech by a Nagasaki hibakusha.

Since moving to Boston in 1985 I have had several opportunities to assist hibakusha speaking tours. I have always enjoyed those visits because they give me a chance to repay a portion of the debt I owe to those who showed me such exquisite hospitality when I was in Japan. It is a privilege to attend their presentations and, afterward, to listen to members of the audience as they grapple with their feelings in response to hibakusha testimony. It is not so much the horror that they remember, but that distinctive "spirit of Hiroshima," which is all the more remarkable in the context of those sharp and terrible memories. I have had these conversations in inner-city high schools and placid suburban churches and many places in between, and I am always moved by the spontaneity and honesty elicited by hibakusha testimony.

It is through these conversations that I came to understand that my passion was not to know the details of what hibakusha suffered, but to try to understand their self-knowledge, their inter-action with outsiders, and how those outsiders have been affected by meeting hibakusha. I needed to know their narratives of suf-fering and survival so that I could leave those charred streets and follow hibakusha on their pilgrimage out to the world.

One of the most vivid moments of my month in Hiroshima occurred when I visited a hibakusha clinic. Before the physician director spoke with me she took me on a tour of the impressive modern facility. It was in the medical records room of that clinic that I finally sensed the immensity of human suffering caused by the bomb. The dozens of shelves of charts incarnated the statis-tics I had read; each chart was an individual and each one testified to the unending nature of radiation's damage. At first I thought that my strong reaction to all those records (more compelling than the powerful exhibits in the Peace Memorial Museum) was due to their volume, but later I realized that those very ordinary folders were the means through which I connected with Hiroshima's story. Books, photographs, drawings, and monuments are important in conveying the history and details of what happened in Hiroshima and Nagasaki, but for all their power and the knowledge they im-part, the viewer remains outside of the experience of hibakusha. But because I, like most people, have similar charts of data sit-ting in hospitals and physicians' offices, charts at once ordinary and uniquely personal, I was able to take my first tentative steps toward empathy with hibakusha.

It is my hope that this book will function like those medical records: specific enough to teach about Hiroshima and Naga-saki, but revealing of the ordinary so as to be universal. That I can do this is the luxury of a writer approaching Hiroshima in 1995, because there is already a voluminous library about Hiroshima. (Even taken together, all these books convey only a very partial tapestry of these complex events.) The classic books have been written: nothing will ever rival John Hersey's *Hiroshima* nor Richard Rhodes's *The Making of the Atomic Bomb,* nor the encyclopedic reference work *Hiroshima and Nagasaki: The Physical, Medical, and Social Effects of the Atomic Bombings.*[3] In these pages I share some of the writings of hibakusha and make mention of the studies conducted by committed professionals — physicians, historians, social scientists, journalists — who have made their life's work a careful documentation of the full scope of the horror of those weapons. I have tried to illuminate a portion of the tapestry rarely seen before through three stories that recount the relationship between hibakusha and American peace activists, the special burdens of American hibakusha, and differences between Hiroshima and Nagasaki.

Hibakusha and American pacifists: My effort to understand the city of Hiroshima was aided by the gift of good teachers; one of these was Barbara Reynolds (1916–90), a religious (evangelical Quaker) pacifist who was granted honorary citizenship by the city of Hiroshima. Barbara Reynolds's autobiography is the story of one woman's transformation from political apathy to activism. Her most intense involvement with hibakusha (1958 to 1978) occurred over a period when there were major changes in the self-perception of hibakusha. Barbara is remembered in Hiroshima for specific acts of charity and her strong stand against nuclear weapons; even more important than her speech and action, she was transformed into a symbolic American, allowing hibakusha the opportunity to negotiate a new type of relationship with Americans.

Barbara and I began corresponding in 1984; we would meet twice, once in 1988, and again the following year. She was particularly generous in sharing insights about her work and helped me to understand the difficulties that mark the path out of historical enmity. We had begun to explore the spirituality of reconciliation when she died, suddenly, in 1990.

American hibakusha: There are an estimated fifteen hundred American hibakusha living in the United States; of these, 40 percent are Japanese women who married American soldiers during the Occupation, 20 percent immigrated normally during the postwar years, and 40 percent are Nisei, first-generation Americans of Japanese descent. It was normal for Issei (immigrant Japanese) parents to send their children to Japan for purposes of education and marriage, and many of them were unable to leave once the war began. Since the largest number of Japanese immigrants to the United States originated from rural areas around Hiroshima, there were many Nisei among those exposed to the atomic bomb. Eventually repatriated to the United States, they have borne an isolation far more extreme than their Japanese or Korean counterparts. The silence they have endured is of a darker texture than that which other hibakusha have borne, because in their attempt to speak on their own behalf (in an effort to attain a small measure of protection against catastrophic medical expenses) they have, once again, engendered accusations (this time by Americans) that they were the "enemy." The story of American hibakusha illuminates the nature of that double-edged sword, loyalty, and reveals how cultural influences determine strategies of social activism.

Nagasaki: When I was in Japan financial and time constraints made it impossible for me to visit Nagasaki, but shortly after I returned to the United States I had the opportunity to review *The Bells of Nagasaki* and was introduced to the writings and spirituality of the Nagasaki hibakusha leader, the physician and writer Takashi Nagai. Nagasaki is a city whose experience of faith has unfolded within a tradition of martyrdom. Dr. Nagai crafted an eloquent understanding of the bomb that was entirely consistent with that history, arguing that Nagasaki was chosen as a "burnt offering," "lambs offered to God in reparation for the sins of the Second World War." While not all Nagasaki hibakusha have embraced Dr. Nagai's spirituality, he had considerable influence on the city's immediate post-war period. Pope John Paul II's 1981 visit to Nagasaki included the ringing denunciation that "war is an act of man, not God." The truth of that declaration does not diminish the heroic witness of Dr. Nagai's faith, a belief in God's loving care that was affirmed in the midst of the nuclear wasteland.

In Hiroshima I interviewed several hibakusha teachers who asked me when, and how, I had learned about the atomic bomb. They were professionally interested in this because of their work in developing peace education curricula, important antidotes to official Ministry of Education textbooks, which consistently and insultingly spread a euphemistic gloss over the realities of World War II. These teachers are convinced that if they are able to convey to their students the full scope of the devastation wreaked by the bomb they can imbue an abhorrence of war in a generation raised in comfort, affluence, and security.

I could never adequately answer their question because I cannot recall when I learned about Hiroshima. Like others of my generation I remember the abrasive sound of air raid sirens and the (patently foolish) drills that had us huddling under our desks or solemnly filing into the school's concrete basement, but I must have had some image of Hiroshima by the time of my early adolescence, some facts around which to crystalize the dread and fear of those hauntingly beautiful October days of the Cuban Missile Crisis.

Regardless of when I learned the facts about Hiroshima, I began to understand the city when I met Jesuit Father Richard McSorley in 1971. Then, as now, a professor of peace studies at Georgetown University, Father McSorley seemed to embody the American radicalism and religious pacifism in which I sought to educate myself. Deeply involved in both the civil rights and anti-war movements, he was well read in the theorists of non-violence, and like Gandhi, whom he delighted in quoting, Father McSorley creatively and courageously conducted "experiments in truth" in his own life.

Father McSorley had a very graphic set of slides about the aftermath of the atomic bomb, and part of his peace work involved lecturing about Hiroshima and Nagasaki, using the slides as evidence to support his eloquent plea that nuclear weapons made ludicrous any possibility of a war being just. I saw his slides on several occasions and found them as shocking as they were reputed to be, but something more important was mediated by the sketchy facts I knew about Father McSorley's personal history.

A Jesuit seminarian studying in the Philippines when the war began, Father McSorley spent the war years as a captive of the Japanese, suffering the violence and abuse that is the common thread of most prisoner of war narratives. He made only elliptical references to that suffering, and what few details I learned were contained in what I suspect were carefully crafted anecdotes, most of them about small but vital psychological victories over the camp's guards. I am sure he carried a pain that few were allowed to see. Despite his activism, he routinely avoided occasions of civil disobedience. (I was in court the day he was arraigned after a sit-in of religious leaders at the U.S. Capitol. He had spent the night in jail, sharing a cell with Benjamin Spock and William Sloane Coffin. He seemed jubilant, as if this arrest and confinement exorcised demons of memory from an earlier, far harsher imprisonment.)

I never heard Father McSorley speak about Hiroshima and his wartime experience at the same time, but having that knowledge about him enhanced the respect I felt as I listened to his passionate denunciation of the atomic bomb. If I accord him the respect of naming him my first teacher about Hiroshima, it is because he limned that city's story with the mystery of forgiveness, preparing me to be receptive to the "spirit of Hiroshima." His absolute refusal to entertain the temptation of seeing the bomb as revenge for his suffering is a stark contrast to those who respond to Hiroshima and Nagasaki with a clenched-teeth litany of Pearl Harbor, Bataan, Okinawa. Meeting Father McSorley prepared me to listen to hibakusha.

My understanding of Hiroshima was strongly influenced by the ethos of the Community for Creative Nonviolence, and so I want to briefly note its biases. In later years CCNV would gain national prominence because of Mitch Snyder's activism on behalf of the homeless, but during the time of my involvement the Community had a rich diversity of members, interests, and activities. The Community educated me to see the consequences of military and political acts through the intimate experiences of the ordinary people whose lives were altered because of those events. Given this background it was perhaps inevitable that my interest in Hiroshima would not be in the realm of politics, science, or history, but in the human story of hibakusha and the way they have shaped their legacy of suffering.

One memorable event the Community organized was a protest during the August 1976 International Eucharistic Congress in Philadelphia. On each day of the Congress the main liturgy honored a particular group of people (youth, parents, clergy, etc.), and, in what was the epitome of insensitive scheduling, the Mass of August 6, the Feast of the Transfiguration — and the anniversary of the bombing of Hiroshima — was dedicated to the military.

The Community learned of this schedule several months prior to the Congress and began a lobbying campaign to urge that, at the very least, the date of the military Mass be changed, but efforts by lay and religious leaders were futile. We spent the week in Philadelphia conducting informational leafletting, and on August 6, after vociferously and vocally expressing opposition to the members of the hierarchy processing into the cathedral, we held an alternative liturgy of remembrance at an inner-city Episcopal church.

In retrospect, the importance of that week was not the display of support for hibakusha, but an episode of remembered fear. Philadelphia was in the grip of anxiety about the illness now known as Legionnaires' disease. The Eucharistic Congress followed by several weeks an American Legion convention; shortly after returning home, some Legionnaires developed severe respiratory symptoms that could follow a rapid course before the patient died. The press in Philadelphia, while taking a generally responsible tone, had nothing substantive to report: all that was known for certain was that the disease was not infectious. Rumors were rife during those hot, uncomfortable weeks, in a city clotted with tens of thousands of international visitors, with no one knowing if the pathogen that had killed these men was airborne or present in water or food. (Some, prone to conspiracy theories, speculated that the government had deliberately released a chemical or biological agent into the environment to test its lethal properties.)

Like a traveler who collects maps and dreams of future journeys, I was given such experiences to prepare me to go to Hiroshima. I would think of the constant, subliminal fear of that week when I learned that, in the aftermath of the bomb, hibakusha were convinced that nothing would grow in Hiroshima again, that the city would be uninhabitable for seventy-five years, and that all who had been exposed to the bomb would be dead within six months. Those rumors, compounded by horrible stories of women aborting hideously deformed fetuses and by exaggerated conclusions drawn from the inexplicable course of acute radiation sickness, created an atmosphere of profound anxiety that would compound the burdens of hibakusha's ill health.

The Community afforded me the opportunity to meet other people like Father McSorley, men and women whose wartime experiences required of them a tenacious understanding of reconciliation. Through an acquaintance I was introduced to Gloria Chou, a U.S. citizen of Chinese birth whom I met with in Tokyo. Her father had been killed by the Japanese, leaving her mother to raise four daughters under the dangerous and oppressive conditions of their occupation. After immigrating to the United States, she spent several years in a religious community, eventually leaving to pursue a career as an educator. She applied for and accepted a two-year teaching position in Tokyo because she wanted to deal with the residue of anger she felt toward the Japanese, work she felt able to do only in Japan. She embarked on this journey not knowing if she would overcome her rage or have it confirmed and deepened. Her courageous, hidden action, because it contained the potential for a profound reconciliation (one forged from an openness to her own pain and a refusal to rely on facile judgments) means that she, like hibakusha, is a peacemaker of profound courage and humility.

There is a Japanese tradition called *o-miyage*, the exchange of souvenirs of travel, which has roots in rural community life at a time when travel was dangerous and difficult, a time before cameras or widespread literacy, when storytelling was a rich part of the fabric of rural community life. When travelers returned safely to their village, it would be cause for celebration, and they would bring with them stories of all they had seen, word portraits of distant places. *O-miyage* has become much more mundane than that, taking its place in the ritualized gift-giving of modern Japanese life, but I am charmed by the romantic delicacy of its origin.

I brought one traditional *o-miyage* with me, in the form of a story I heard from an artist friend, Marguerite Fletcher. We were discussing the differences between personal and historical reconciliation, and in the course of our conversation she told me the story about her childhood in a small Oregon farming community, "a hospitable mix of cultures and religions." I asked Marguerite to write the story out for me so that I could take it to Japan, and she was kind enough to oblige.

When her paternal grandfather died, her family inherited a beautiful old Japanese porcelain vase, which Marguerite especially treasured. One day her father gave it to a Japanese family in the community, explaining only "they will appreciate it more than we ever could." It was an excuse that, to her, never compensated for the loss of its beauty.

She was a child, and therefore ignorant about the relocation of Japanese families during the war. Later she learned about what happened and heard stories about neighbors protecting the land and possessions of the Japanese. Telling me the story, she wondered if those "gentle heroics" were idealized, but thought they were at least partially true, "otherwise the aftermath of the war could not have been so full of sweet communion." Telling the story, she realized, for the first time, that her father's gift of the vase "was an act of reparation, of regret, of restoration, of repentance. The words are inadequate. They speak too loudly, too consciously, of a gesture which perhaps came from all of them but, then again, certainly from none of them. The gift was a gift of recognition and reverence ... his *was* a racial gesture. Racial reverence replacing, reversing racial paranoia. The gift was a simple and spontaneous act reflecting an honest movement of the heart. I also know that it was an act of reconciliation."

I brought that story to Hiroshima, and when I met Yoko Ninomiya, I knew that she was the person I was meant to give it to. A young woman, the daughter of a hibakusha, she took me to visit the tranquil Buddhist temple Mitaki (the word means three waterfalls) on the outskirts of Hiroshima. Afterward, we went to her home for lunch, and she showed me her father's garden; because land is precious in urbanized Japan (being both scarce and expensive) his garden had been planted on the steep slope of a hill that extended to the edge of their property. No one else in the family helped him with his garden, which he patiently tended on his rare days off from his job with the Japan National Railway. Later, she told me the outlines of her father's A-bomb story, of how he had found his parents dead in the ruins of their home and of how he had cremated them in what had once been their equally beautiful garden.

Her father was a silent hibakusha, a man whose post-war life was, by its very ordinary anonymity, a rebuke to the demonic power of radiation. He did not speak publicly about his experiences, did not travel to demonstrations in Japan or abroad, had never joined peace or hibakusha organizations. He was, by nature, a private man, reticent about his wartime experiences even within his family. Yet he became, for me, an eloquent spokesman for the resiliency of the human spirit. It was in his garden that I felt an upsurge of hope that possibly there would be (in the slogan of the peace groups) "no more Hiroshimas, no more Nagasakis, no more hibakusha." Its beauty was a proclamation, by one hibakusha, that nuclear war was not inevitable, because it would be madness to believe that it was and still spend thirty years patiently nurturing a garden of such abundant beauty, a garden that became for me an utterly unambiguous, clear, dogmatic, and eloquent statement of hope.

I gave Marguerite's story to Yoko — partly because it was a story about a father and a daughter, but mainly because I wanted to find a small way to honor Yoko and the work she has chosen to do, to cultivate friendships across national and cultural boundaries. In similar ways this book is an *o-miyage* — the story, not of nuclear destruction, but of the resilience of the human spirit and the unexpected finding of silent gifts.

1

City of Silence and Hope

HIROSHIMA

—— ∞ ——

The strangest thing was the silence. It was one of the most un-forgettable impressions I have. You'd think that people would be panic-stricken, running, yelling. Not at Hiroshima. They moved in slow motion, like figures in a silent movie, shuffling through the dust and smoke. I heard thousands of people breathing the words, "Water, give me water." Many simply dropped to the ground and died.

— Setsuko Thurlow

... the silence in the grove by the river, where hundreds of grue-somely wounded suffered together, was one of the most dreadful and awesome phenomena of his whole experience. The hurt ones were quiet: no one wept, much less screamed in pain; no one com-plained: none of the many who died did so noisily; not even the children cried; very few people even spoke. And when Father Klein-sorge gave water to some whose faces had been almost blotted out by flash burns, they took their share and then raised themselves a little and bowed to him, in thanks.

— John Hersey, Hiroshima

Hiroshima is a city of silence that contains within itself many kinds of silence.

The city of Hiroshima was attacked by a uranium-fueled atomic bomb at 8:15 on the morning of Monday, August 6, 1945. The day was hot and humid and the sky over Hiroshima was clear. On August 9, a plutonium atomic bomb was dropped over the port city of Nagasaki, on the island of Kyushu, at 11:02 in the morning.[1] Six days later Emperor Hirohito informed his subjects that Japan had accepted the terms of surrender set forth in the Potsdam Dec-laration. The despair that greeted this announcement was felt with particular acuity in Hiroshima and Nagasaki: one of the few things that had sustained the severely injured victims was the hope of Japanese retaliation for the terrible attack. With the surrender, fifteen years of war and military rule ended and the subsequent seven-year Allied Occupation ushered in major social changes:

> a redistribution of the land, the democratization of education, the legalization of labor unions and the break-up of the great business corporations or *zaibatsu*. There was also the new and democratic Constitution which, among other changes such as renouncing war, officially abolished the old patriarchal family system and gave women full political and civil rights on an equal basis with men.[2]

The Pacific War has long been over for most Japanese, who have enjoyed the fruits of post-war prosperity, but it has never ended for hibakusha. There are actually two Chinese characters for *baku*, the root of "hibakusha." One character reads *baku* as "explode," which yields "hibakusha" as one who is bombed (subjected to a bombing or an explosion). The other character for *baku* means "expose" and yields "hibakusha" as one exposed to radiation. It is this second definition that has allowed the hibakusha of Hiroshima and Nagasaki to extend the appellation to later victims of radiation's ravages: uranium miners, people living "downwind" from atmospheric nuclear tests, atomic veterans, and residents of Chernobyl, Three Mile Island, and the Marshall Islands. This identification with a broader community has lessened their feelings of isolation and allowed them to communicate what they have learned through five decades of living with radiation.

The lessons of Hiroshima and Nagasaki are both political and personal — personal because hibakusha are, in the words of the Japanese essayist Kenzaburo Oe, "unsurrendered," "authentic human beings...who have neither too little nor too much hope, who never surrender to any situation but courageously carry on with their day-to-day tasks."[3] There are also political lessons to be wrested from a study of the atomic bomb, for it is in the public arena that hibakusha have attempted to seek meaning in their survival. That they survived is inexplicable to many hibakusha: why did I survive, they ask, when so many others died? Neither their personal nor their public struggles have been free from conflict, but an observer who views the panorama of words and images, symbols and actions that are hibakusha's legacy, can only be humbled by its patterns of resilience and hope.

The proper Japanese name for the atom bomb is *genbaku* (*gen*=half of *genshi* for "atom" and *baku*=half of *bakudan* for bomb), but survivors, who had no knowledge of atomic energy, first called it by the strangely comforting diminutive, *pika-don*.

Pika means flash, and *don* means boom. Survivors saw the flash and heard the boom, and some have commented on an eerie, palpable silence when the mushroom cloud ascended over Hiroshima. An estimated 130,000 people died in Hiroshima and 60,000–70,000 in Nagasaki; while the majority of victims were Japanese, there were tens of thousands of non-Japanese resident in Japan who were exposed to or died in the bombings. The majority of these were Korean, but there were also Americans, Chinese, and Allied war prisoners among the casualties. In 1985, there were 367,000 people who met the Japanese government's legal definition of hibakusha: people who were in Hiroshima and Nagasaki at the time of the bombing, early entrants to the city (within a two-week period when there were significant levels of residual radiation), those who were exposed to radiation through handling heavily irradiated survivors (medical relief workers and those who disposed of corpses) and fetal survivors, those exposed in utero.[4] The above casualty statistics are only estimates, as are the wartime population figures for Hiroshima and Nagasaki. Significant population shifts took place during the war, with an influx of military personnel and civilian defense employees and an evacuation of both the very young and very old to outlying rural areas. The above statistics include deaths through December 1945; after that date, fatalities from acute radiation sickness had begun to abate. To be accurate, casualty statistics have to include the hibakusha who, to this very day, are dying from radiation-related diseases. This is the categorical difference between atomic and conventional weapons; they are not simply more powerful, but because they emit massive doses of radiation they are weapons that kill through time.

Strategists and historians have debated whether the use of the atomic bombs were necessary to achieve an American victory.[5] President Truman's stated justification is supported by many Americans: the atomic bombings hastened the end of the war, thus saving the hundreds of thousands of American and Japanese lives that would have been lost had the Allies invaded the Japanese mainland. By now, however, most historians have concluded that the bombs were not militarily necessary because Japan had already begun negotiations over the terms of surrender; months of saturation bombing had decimated their material and moral ability to continue the war effort. The Air Force acknowledged as much in its June 1946 Strategic Bombing Survey:

> The further question of the effects of the bombs on the morale of the Japanese leaders and their decision to abandon the war is tied up with other factors. The atomic bomb had more effect on the thinking of Government leaders than on

the morale of the rank and file of civilians outside of the target areas. It cannot be said, however, that the atomic bomb convinced the leaders who effected the peace of the necessity of surrender. The decision to seek ways and means to terminate the war, influenced in part by knowledge of the low state of popular morale, had been taken in May 1945 by the Supreme War Guidance Council.[6]

The atomic bombings were partially motivated by political considerations, intended to be a warning to the Soviet Union and a statement of American dominance of post-war geopolitics. At the Yalta Conference the Allies had agreed that the Soviet Union would enter the war against Japan three months after Germany's defeat; they did so on August 8, 1945, and were making rapid advances against Japanese troops in China. The use of the atomic bombs was meant to insure that Americans would control the Occupation of Japan. The lack of a clear military necessity for the use of the atomic bombs led to hibakusha's outrage and a sense of having been violated in a scientific experiment. Some hibakusha believe that there was a strong racial component to the decision to drop the bomb and question whether it would have been used against a white European enemy.[7]

The American press portrayed the atomic bombs as powerful weapons (emphasizing their destructive power in comparison to TNT) that had been used for good ends, but paid scant attention to the human cost of their use. There was a notable absence of information about the immediate and long-term effects of radiation exposure. "Everything the American people learned about the bombing from its newspapers on August 7, and for days and weeks to come, had been prepared for it by the War Department, which set and controlled the journalistic agenda during those first crucial moments of the atomic age."[8] It was not until September 3 that American reporters were able to visit Hiroshima. The reporters, who had been selected by the military, were closely chaperoned during their time there. Their reports differed from that of Wilfred Burchett, the first independent reporter to reach Hiroshima. Burchett, an Australian newspaperman for the British *Daily Express,* was shocked by the extent of the city's destruction but also wrote about survivors dying from a mysterious disease that he called an "atomic plague."[9]

Hiroshima ("broad island") is a flat, fan-shaped delta city, surrounded on three sides by hills and on the fourth by the Seto Inland Sea. The Ota River, which flows south from the Chugoku Mountains, divides into six branches in the city before it empties into Hiroshima Bay. An established town center during the Edo period

(1603–1868), Hiroshima became more prosperous and important during the years of modernization under the Meiji emperor. As the seat of regional government for Hiroshima Prefecture, the city was home to many cultural, political, and educational institutions; it had been an important regional military center since the Sino-Japanese War in 1894. The city's Ujina Harbor, completed in 1889, allowed Hiroshima to develop a lucrative commercial shipping industry, and it grew to become the eighth largest city in Hiroshima Prefecture. During the Pacific War it was the point of embarkation for troops and supplies of the Second Army, which was headquartered in Hiroshima. There was a large naval shipyard and munitions factory in nearby Kure, fifteen kilometers away.

City officials and residents, aware of Hiroshima's strategic importance, were somewhat anxious about their safety, since other, less significant cities, had experienced bombing raids. In anticipation of such raids they undertook preventive measures, including the evacuation of young children and the elderly, the mobilization of thousands of older school children, who were put to work tearing down houses in the center of the city to create firebreaks, and the institution of extensive civil defense and emergency medical procedures. Nervous citizens proposed several theories to explain their safety: some thought that Hiroshima was spared because the United States respected it as the home prefecture of its Japanese immigrant community. Other explanations were more fanciful, such as the belief that President Truman was attracted to the physical beauty of Hiroshima and planned to live or vacation there after the war; a variation of this rumor held that his mother was secretly living in Hiroshima. Still other people suspected the truth, that Hiroshima had been singled out for attack by a terrible new weapon. Once Hiroshima was placed on the list of atomic bomb target cities, it was spared conventional attack to insure an accurate assessment of the bomb's damage.

August 6, 1945

The bomb exploded in the air about 600 meters above the city.

At the moment of explosion, a fireball with a temperature of several million degrees centigrade and an atmospheric pressure of several hundred thousand bars was formed at the burst point. The fireball rapidly expanded to a sphere with a maximum radius of about 230 meters, emitted particularly strong thermal rays until three seconds after the explosion, and continued to shine for about ten seconds. Because of the thermal rays, the temperature of the hypocenter [the surface position directly beneath the center of the nuclear explosion] is thought to have risen to 3,000–4,000 degrees centigrade — far higher than the temperature at which iron melts, 1,550 degrees centigrade.

The strong expansive power of the fireball produced what is known as a shock wave, followed by a high-speed wind. The pressure that occurs at the burst point of an atomic bomb creates a wave of air that travels at supersonic velocity. The amount of this shock wave's pressure in excess of atmospheric pressure is called the overpressure of the blast. . . . The pressure from the shock wave at Hiroshima was extremely destructive, its overpressure reaching about thirty-six metric tons per square meter at the hypocenter. . . .

Buildings were smashed to pieces and incinerated by the blast and thermal rays, and it was the great quantities of dust from the destroyed buildings, carried by the winds, that cast the city into pitch-darkness just after the bombing.[10]

The heat at ground zero was so intense that vital organs were vaporized and death was almost instantaneous. Burns from thermal rays caused damage to deep tissues. Many people suffered from both primary thermal burns and secondary burns from the fires caused by the bomb's intense heat. Victims were trapped beneath wooden structures that collapsed from the blast or experienced trauma (bruises, cuts, and fractures) from flying debris. These wounds became severely infected because of the decrease in resistance secondary to radiation exposure.

With a violent flash that ripped the sky apart and a thunderous sound that shook the earth to its foundation, Hiroshima was pounded to the ground in an instant. Then, from where a whole city once was, a huge column of fire bounded straight up toward heaven. A dense cloud of smoke rose and spread out, covering and darkening the whole sky. The earth below became shrouded in heavy darkness. The dead and wounded lay fallen, piled up, everywhere: the carnage was like a scene in hell. Then, fires broke out all over and soon merged into a huge conflagration, which grew in intensity moment by moment. As a fierce whirlwind blew, half-naked and stark naked bodies, darkly soiled and covered with blood, began moving; in clustered groups resembling departed spirits, they staggered away in bewildered flight from the inferno. One after another fell down and died. Countless others lay trapped under fallen debris and were burned alive; their pa-

thetic voices calling for family members, and for help, could
be heard within the wildly dancing flames. . . .

When their hands hung down, the blood accumulated
in the fingertips and caused throbbing pain, so they held
their arms up and forward; burned so badly that the skin
peeled and hung loosely, their raw hands and arms oozed and
dripped blood. They looked just like ghosts. Barely managing
not to fall over, they stumbled along in continuous lines to
escape from fiery death.[11]

The bomb's initial radiation, emitted within one minute of the
explosion, was comprised of alpha and beta particles, gamma
rays and neutrons; when the neutrons of these radioactive particles reached the ground they were absorbed by the soil and other
substances. This induced radioactivity, combined with atmospheric
fallout, resulted in residual radiation. There were significant levels of residual radiation for three days after the bombs fell, and
thus early entrants (rescue workers and people who entered to
look for relatives) are also considered hibakusha. The total dose
of radiation exposure is determined by several factors: distance
from the hypocenter, if one was outside or inside at the time of
the explosion and, if inside, whether the building was made of
steel, concrete, brick, or wood (earth and concrete provide some
protection against gamma rays).

Throughout the day, a tower-shaped cloud hung over the
city, and from 9:00 in the morning until 4:00 in the afternoon
"black rain" fell "in large, muddy, sticky, pitch-black drops, coarse
enough to give pain to the naked bombing victims."[12] This black
rain contained radioactive debris, soot, and residue from fires, and
the pattern of wind and rainfall increased the circumference of
radiation exposure.[13]

Ninety percent of Hiroshima's physical structures (most of
which were wooden) were destroyed by the blast effect and fire-
storm. Police, fire, communications, transportation, and medical
services, essential for the care of survivors, were rendered use-
less. Ninety percent of medical personnel were dead or disabled;
eighteen emergency hospitals and thirty-two first aid clinics were
destroyed, but surviving medical personnel (despite their own injuries and a lack of drugs and equipment) were heroic in providing
emergency care.

My clothes were tattered and covered with blood. I had cuts
and scratches all over me, but all of my extremities were
there. I looked around me. Even though it was morning, the
sky was dark, as dark as twilight. Then I saw streams of
human beings shuffling away from the center of the city. Parts

of their bodies were missing. Their eyes had been liquefied. They had blackened skin, and strips of flesh hung like ribbons from their bones. There was an awful stench in the air; the stench of burnt human flesh. I can't describe that smell, but it was a bit like broiled fish.[14]

People fleeing from the city made their way to outlying rural areas. Fire boats were used to bring over ten thousand severely wounded survivors to Ninoshima, a sparsely populated island (seventeen hundred residents) four kilometers south of Hiroshima Port. On August 7 military and civilian relief workers from outlying areas were mobilized to bring in food, set up emergency medical stations, and begin the weeks-long process of cremating and disposing of the tens of thousands of corpses that clogged the city streets and floated in the rivers. These rescuers and military and government workers performed extraordinary feats in rapidly restoring public service to the city: clearing roads and rail lines and re-establishing train service, electrical power, and postal and telephone operations.

In corpses near ground zero the eyeballs were blown outside their heads. The skin was a black-tinged yellowish brown, and very dry; it was clear that these persons had died in agony. Whether they were incinerated instantly by the intense heat, or were crushed by the immense blast force, theirs was an instant death from a sudden flash and blast of proportions beyond imagination.... Many corpses were found at places where there was water — rivers, old wells, cisterns, ponds and the like. Persons who did not die instantly had, it appears, exerted themselves to the limit in their search for water.

As the days passed, our main job become disposal of corpses.... Ashes and bone remains of unidentifiable corpses were gathered in each local district and buried in temporary graves, on which were placed simple markers. Identifiable remains were sorted out to give to surviving families, but no one came to receive some of these remains.[15]

It was several days before the nature of the new weapon was understood, and even then "the knowledge that it was the atomic bomb that had exploded was no help to us at all from a medical standpoint, as no one in the world knew its full effects on the human organism. We were, in effect, the first guinea pigs in such experimentation."[16]

Radiation penetrates deeply into the human body and injures the cells constituting the body. When radiation penetrates a cell, ionization and release of energy result in damage of molecules or of molecular groups. . . .

The sensitivity of human cells varies from one cell to the other. In general, actively regenerating and proliferating cells are most sensitive to radiation. Young blood cells (hemoblast cells or proliferating blood cells in bone marrow), lymphocytes, mucosal epithelial cells of the intestine, spermatogonia of the testicles, and follicle cells of the ovaries are considered the most radiosensitive cells. These are followed in sensitivity by mucosal epithelial cells of the mouth, of the esophagus, of the stomach, epithelial cells of the eye lens, and cells forming the hair bulb.[17]

The symptoms of acute radiation sickness reflect this sensitivity: on the day of the bombing, people experienced nausea, vomiting, and loss of appetite. Within the first weeks survivors noted bloody diarrhea, purpura (bleeding into the skin), and loss of hair. Lesions and ulcers of the mouth and throat, a decrease in white blood cells, and anemia were noted up to the first month, along with high fevers, infection, and an accompanying malaise. When medical tests were done, these people were found to have severe abnormalities in white cell and platelet counts. Thermal burns eventually healed into disfiguring, crippling keloid scars. These rope-like, deep scars are one of the most common visual reminders of the bomb, and many hibakusha required surgery to remove the scars and regain function of affected limbs.

The Strategic Bombing Survey provided chilling testimony to "the awesome lethal effects of the atomic bomb and the insidious additional peril of the gamma rays":

> There is reason to believe that if the effects of blast and fire had been entirely absent from the bombing, the number of deaths among people within a radius of one-half mile from ground zero would have been almost as great as the actual figures and the deaths among those within 1 mile would have been only slightly less. The principal difference would have been in the time of the deaths. Instead of being killed outright as were most of these victims, they would have survived for a few days or even 3 or 4 weeks, only to die eventually of radiation disease.[18]

Survivors, sick, frightened, ignorant about radiation, saw that even people who had escaped the city without visible injuries died, and from this they came to believe three rumors: it was said that anyone who had been in Hiroshima on August 6 would soon die; that the city would be uninhabitable for seventy-five years; that nothing would ever grow again in Hiroshima.

One accepted his doom when he found his hairs begin to drop and the gums to bleed between the teeth. My wife reported to me when she revisited the city on the first of September, that men there were exchanging greetings as they met, saying, "Haven't your hairs fallen out yet?" This was literally a "Greeting of Death."[19]

The winter of 1945 was particularly harsh; the severe weather seemed to mirror the stark poverty and physical suffering of hibakusha, but the following spring was marked by a lush growth of vegetation (almost frighteningly verdant because of radiation), and in this regeneration of nature survivors embraced a metaphor for the possibility of restoration in their personal and communal lives.

The Aftermath

The city of Hiroshima likens itself to a Phoenix that rose from the ashes of atomic devastation, but it is easier to rebuild a city than to refashion lives that were shattered by the overwhelming destruction of the bomb. The bomb killed people, but it also decimated the fabric of family life, community groups, neighborhoods, and social rituals. Private and communal property and wealth, places of employment, bank accounts, possessions, food, clothing, shelter, municipal records, and city services vanished. It was the extent of this destruction that led hibakusha to think of the bomb, not so much as a weapon of war, but as an act of nature. They accepted it with resignation, much as they would a typhoon or earthquake.

Hibakusha speak of the "keloid of the heart" and "leukemia of the spirit" to denote the affliction of emotional suffering that is deeper than even the physical ravages of radiation. For many hibakusha, the persistent recurrence of memories of "that day" is compounded by despair that they had failed to rescue members of their family.

Heightened press and public attention to Hiroshima during the weeks leading up to the annual commemoration service can precipitate a recurrence of hibakusha's memories and fears, but so can reading a newspaper article that reports a nuclear weapons test or the development of new generations of weapons systems or that quotes a bellicose world leader threatening their use. The continuation of the arms race has been an "intolerable spiritual burden" for hibakusha. Some hibakusha have combatted their depression through involvement in anti-nuclear protests and education of young students. They ache to communicate the truth of their experiences and strive to "preserve the memory of war" so that all people will "realize that the abolishment of nuclear weapons is necessary for the preservation of the human race."[20]

Hibakusha have known no antidote to an almost constant anxiety about the insidious permutations of radiation's impact on human health. Diseases attributed to radiation have spread throughout the hibakusha community with depressing regularity. Leukemia and other blood disorders were first noted in 1947; atomic cataracts began to be diagnosed the following year. In the late 1960s laboratory studies first revealed chromosome abnormalities in hibakusha, but the significance of this finding is still unknown. By 1970 researchers noted that hibakusha had notably increased incidences of solid tumor cancers of the breast, thyroid, salivary glands, lungs, and stomach. They have also had a markedly decreased resistance to infection and require prolonged recuperation after surgery. Many hibakusha have known a persistent, low-level debilitation and malaise that they attribute to "A-bomb sickness."

Hibakusha's greatest anxiety is reserved for the still unanswered question: given radiation's known mutagenic effect, what impact did their radiation exposure have on their children? This fear was given voice in early rumors about survivors who miscarried hideously deformed fetuses (there was a transient increase in miscarriages and fetal mortality of women exposed to the atomic bombs). There were no medical studies of second-generation hibakusha until the 1970s; to date there has been no indication that they have increased rates of radiation-related diseases.

Japanese law provided two months of medical relief for wartime casualties, and no exception was made for the severely injured hibakusha. Relief centers in Hiroshima and Nagasaki were closed in October 1945, after which the emotionally exhausted, financially destitute, and desperately ill hibakusha were required to obtain and pay for their own medical care. In the fall of 1945, as hibakusha slowly returned to the sites that had once been their home, they found themselves a demographic minority in Hiroshima. Healthy, non-hibakusha Hiroshima residents and outsiders (including demobilized soldiers) took advantage of both hibakusha's physical weakness and the destruction of tax and property records to create in post-war Hiroshima something almost unknown in Japan: the rough, exhilarating atmosphere of a frontier town.

The rending of the bonds of family life made it impossible for many hibakusha to regain their pre-bomb physical or emotional vitality. Many families suffered the loss of the breadwinner, and if the surviving parent was disabled, children were required to assume major caregiver responsibilities. Over five thousand children were orphaned by the bomb, and a fragile social service network

could care for only a small number of them. (Teachers and Buddhist priests opened a residence for orphans in late 1945.) Many
children lived in gangs near the railway station and supported
themselves through the black market and other illegal activities.
The early physical and emotional deprivation experienced by these
children spiraled into discrimination during their adult years because a lack of family ties hampered them in obtaining favorable
education and employment opportunities.

The loneliness of the orphaned children was mirrored by that
endured by the "orphaned elderly," those who lost spouses and
children to the bomb. Many were women who, to provide for
themselves, worked as low-paid day laborers rather than accept
government relief. The comparatively high percentage of hibakusha day laborers was partially due to economic discrimination;
employers assumed that hibakusha would be poor employees because of recurrent medical problems. Hibakusha have also suffered
discrimination in marriage because of fears that radiation exposure would result in genetic damage to future generations. Japan is
a society fiercely conscious of familial lineage, and it is not surprising that hibakusha would be considered poor marriage partners.
Despite being gripped by this vicious cycle of disease, poverty,
and discrimination, hibakusha have continued to display a tenacious moral courage: perhaps the greatest sign of hope to emerge
from Hiroshima are the countless hibakusha who have married
and borne children.

We remember Hiroshima through its images of destruction —
grotesque burns, keloid scars, hideously splayed flesh wounds —
and wish to avert our eyes. The common response to Hiroshima is
similar to the experience of the British composer Malcolm Williamson. Williamson visited Hiroshima in preparation for writing a
score based on the Edmund Blunden poem "Hiroshima, A Song
for August 6, 1949." Two hibakusha spoke with him; one had
been active in the peace movement, traveling and speaking widely
about her experiences, but the other had been silent, a silence imposed by long years of illness. In addition to visible keloid scars,
radiation exposure had caused breast cancer, necessitating bilateral
mastectomies and subsequent radiation therapy that destroyed her
chest wall. The second hibakusha told Williamson that she envied
hibakusha who could work for peace but all she could do was tell
her story and show her chest wall; after a brief glance the composer
flinched and said, "Enough." This inability to look at Hiroshima
has led to the situation described by the late Swedish diplomat
Olaf Palme — "for all peoples in the world, Hiroshima is, today,
already both myth and reality."

Myths can be either the symbolic representation or the deliberate falsification of truth, and both meanings of the word apply to Hiroshima. One etiology of its fallacious myth was the seven years of institutional censorship during the Allied Occupation of Japan. American press reports may have been written through a prism of political control, but a far more effective censorship was imposed on the Japanese. On September 19, 1945, a Press Code was issued with the laudable "objective of establishing freedom of the press in Japan." It stated, in part:

> (2) Nothing shall be printed which might, directly or by inference, disturb the public tranquility. (3) There shall be no false or destructive criticism of the Allied Powers. (4) There shall be no destructive criticism of the Allied Forces of Occupation and nothing which might invite mistrust or resentment of those troops. (8) Minor details of a news story must not be overemphasized to stress or develop any propaganda line.

"Designed to educate the press of the Japanese in the responsibilities and meaning of a free press," the Press Code emphasized "the truth of news and the elimination of propaganda." Its restrictions applied to "news, editorials and advertisements of all newspapers and will cover, in addition, all publications printed in Japan."[21] The Press Code was particularly insidious because writers were not allowed to mention censorship, nor was there any indication of what material had been censored. In practical terms "all publications" included poetry, essays, novels, photographs, medical information, and hibakusha testimony in both manuscript and published format.

The Press Code imposed a terrible isolation on hibakusha. Japanese scientists and physicians were required to obtain Allied permission to conduct studies about the atomic bomb and were forbidden to publish the results of their research. Hibakusha were denied factual information about the medical consequences of the bomb and were hampered in their ability to understand their continued losses. There were restrictions applied to articles that stressed the human cost of the atomic bomb, writing that could have elicited much needed international financial and emotional support and would have done much to meet hibakusha's physical needs and ameliorate their profound communal and personal loneliness. (There were exceptions to this isolation: in October 1947 physicians from Kyoto University began offering free medical examinations to hibakusha. In April 1948 Hawaiian emigrants from Hiroshima initiated a relief campaign that, within a year, raised $110,000 for hibakusha.) Increasing Cold War tensions, particularly after the 1950 onset of the Korean War, led to a tightening of restrictions against public discussions about the atom bomb.

The most visible American presence in Hiroshima and Naga-
saki was the facilities of the Atomic Bomb Casualty Commission
(ABCC), which was established by order of President Truman in
November 1946. Under the auspices of the National Academy of
Sciences, ABCC was authorized to study the delayed effects of
radiation exposure. (In 1975 ABCC was replaced with the joint
U.S.-Japan Radiation Effects Research Foundation [RERF].) As a
research facility, rather than a diagnostic and treatment center,
ABCC became a magnet for hibakusha's anger at having been used
as medical and scientific guinea pigs. (The non-treatment policy
was partly determined in cooperation with Japanese physicians —
naturally anxious to avoid direct competition with American doctors.[22]) In the 1950s and 1960s, ABCC carried out an aggressive
autopsy program that was particularly resented; not only were au-
topsies alien to Japanese tradition but they were perceived as a
final, ultimate violation of hibakusha, painfully symbolic of the entire atomic bomb experience.[23] Despite this, most hibakusha have
co-operated with ABCC researchers, whether from a respect for
the quality of ABCC's scientific rigor, an ingrained obedience to
authority (as Robert Lifton suggests in *Death in Life*), or because
involvement in medical research affirms their sense of mission.

ABCC was callously duplicitous toward the parents of fetal hibakusha. An estimated 1,608 people were exposed to the bomb
in utero; those pregnant women who had received the highest
dosage of radiation exposure gave birth to infants with severe
microcephaly (small head size) and associated mental and physical retardation. For many years ABCC researchers led parents to
believe that their children's medical problems were due to malnu-
trition because of wartime food shortages during their pregnancy.
It was not until October 1965 that crusading journalists revealed
that retardation was due to radiation exposure, and the angry parents organized Kinoko-kai ("Mushroom Club") to lobby for the
inclusion of their children under hibakusha medical relief law. This
was granted in 1967.

There were some heroic politically radical poets and novelists
who published despite the Press Code, even if it meant privately
printing and distributing their work. Women writers, including
Sadako Kurihara, Shinoe Shoda, and Yoko Ohta, all of whom
had opposed Japanese militarism, persisted in giving voice to hibakusha's pain. Kurihara was the editor of the monthly magazine
Chugoku Bunka (Culture of Chugoku); its first issue was devoted
to writings about the bomb.

Collections of personal A-bomb accounts were published in
both Hiroshima and Nagasaki but were subject to deletions and
delays because of the Press Code. The first such Japanese collection

was *A Voice from Heaven,* compiled by members of the Hiroshima YMCA in 1947 and published two years later. (A second Japanese reprint appeared in 1983, and a 1985 English translation has not been published.) Occupation restrictions against political expressions were tightened with the intensification of the Cold War, and "authorities prohibited the discussion of the atomic bombings at public meetings."

> But on October 2, 1949, at a meeting in the auditorium of Hiroshima Jogakuin a Grade 5 boy stood up unexpectedly, related the loss of his older brother in the atomic bombing and expressed his desire for a world free of atomic bombs. A woman jumped up and, regardless of the possibility of persecution by the Occupation, proposed an emergency resolution appealing to the world to abolish all atomic weapons. This resolution struck a responsive chord in the hearts of the long-repressed citizens and was enthusiastically and unanimously passed. This was the first such appeal made at a public meeting in all Japan and may be considered to be the real birth of the Japanese anti-nuclear movement.[24]

Attempts were made to invoke the Press Code to prevent the August 1946 *New Yorker* publication of John Hersey's *Hiroshima.* (Hersey wrote a fortieth anniversary sequel for the *New Yorker* and a revised edition of the book was published in 1985, which elicits the major themes of Hiroshima's post-war story.) Hersey's skilled narration of the experiences of six hibakusha transformed the stereotyped enemy of wartime propaganda into human beings, faces interposed on casualty statistics. Ironically, for all of the acclaim that justly greeted *Hiroshima,* its "almost elegiac mood" may have functioned to allow readers to "confront emotionally what had happened." Rather than stirring people to action, Hersey's prose leaves the reader "with the feeling that he has gained a deeper understanding of war's human meaning, and through understanding, emotional release."[25]

Funds for reconstruction became available in 1949 after the passage of laws making Hiroshima a Peace Memorial and Nagasaki an International Culture City. Hiroshima's material and moral reconstruction was inspired by the vision and efforts of Shinzo Hamai, its first popularly elected mayor. Mayor Hamai, who was born and raised in Hiroshima and educated at the prestigious Tokyo Imperial University, was in his late thirties at the time of the bombing, a city employee responsible for wartime food distribution. He was exposed to the bomb at his home (approximately three kilometers from the hypocenter) and immediately rushed to City Hall. The building was in flames, the mayor was dead, and senior offi-

cials were incapacitated, and so he simply took over. Robert Lifton
calls him the city's "great post-bomb provider," responsible for obtaining the basic necessities of survival, from food and blankets
to emergency medical relief supplies. Mayor Hamai had a "fierce
loyalty to the geographic site of the city" and a passionate commitment to solving hibakusha problems, but Lifton identifies his
greatest contribution as stemming from his prodigious "talent for
what might be called psychohistorical mediation to the painful decisions Hiroshima was required to make about the problem of
memorializing the bomb" — decisions that balanced international
interest in Hiroshima, the complex feelings of hibakusha, and civic
and economic pressures.[26]

One example of those contentious controversies was the inscription on the A-bomb Cenotaph, which was unveiled in 1952. The
Cenotaph, which is shaped like the clay figure of an ancient house,
hovers protectively over a black stone coffin that includes the reg-
istry of names of all those who have died from the bomb. The
inscription on the front of the coffin reads "Let All the Souls Here
Rest in Peace; For We Shall Not Repeat the Evil." Written by Ta-
dayoshi Saika, a professor at Hiroshima University, it expressed
Mayor Hamai's sentiment "that the over 200,000 victims were not
only the representatives of one nation or one race, but of the whole
world, and they should be recognized as a foundation of peace for
all human beings. All the people on the earth should make this
pledge for a peace without nuclear weapons."[27]

Not everyone concurred that this was a suitable statement; some
people were angered by what they took to be the implicit suggestion that it was the Japanese people who were referred to as the
"We" in the statement. Professor Saika clarified his words by explaining that "the citizens of Hiroshima are not brooding on the
past, but seeking for light toward the future....It is the privilege
of Hiroshima and Nagasaki to resolve that we shall not repeat
this evil. If the efforts of Hiroshima brighten the future for all
human beings, then the sacrifice made by the victims has not been
in vain."[28]

The impoverished hibakusha community had an urgent need for
medical care, but public campaigns on their behalf could not be
organized until after Occupation ended on April 28, 1952, when
the San Francisco Peace Treaty between Japan and the United
States went into effect. In June 1952, Hiroshima civic leaders and
members of the Japan P.E.N. Club (Poets, Essayists and Novelists) undertook a campaign for medical treatment for hibakusha.
The following month, Hiroshima surgeons agreed to provide free
treatment for needy hibakusha. In 1953 A-bomb Casualty Councils
were formed in both Nagasaki and Hiroshima to research medical

effects of the bomb and to embark on a nationwide campaign to raise funds for needy hibakusha.

Remembering

The event that finally focused public attention on hibakusha took place, not in Hiroshima or Nagasaki, but 160 kilometers east of Bikini Island. On March 1, 1954, the crew and cargo of the Japanese boat *Fukuryu Maru No. 5* (it translates, ironically, into "Lucky Dragon No. 5"), which was fishing outside the restricted test zone, was exposed to radioactive fallout from an American hydrogen bomb test being carried out in the Marshall Islands. (Two hundred and sixty-seven Marshall Islanders were also contaminated by radiation, but they received immediate and aggressive medical attention.) The crew remained on the boat for two weeks, during which time they ate from its contaminated tuna cargo, and by the time they returned to their home port in Shizuoka Prefecture, most of the twenty-three crew members were suffering from acute radiation sickness. Aikichi Kuboyama, the boat's chief radio operator, died from complications of radiation exposure on September 23.

The anger that crystallized around the "Lucky Dragon" incident led to an almost spontaneous anti-nuclear movement in Japan; by October 1954 organizers had gathered 14 million signatures on a petition to prohibit the use of atomic weapons. (The nature of the peace movement changed from this grassroots orientation in 1960, when well-funded Communist and Socialist ideologues gained control of the major organizations to stage massive confrontations with the Japanese government over the revision of the Japan-U.S. security treaty. In 1963, at the Ninth World Congress Against Atomic and Hydrogen Bombs, held in Hiroshima, the once-unified peace movement split into three factions.)

The Japanese public was both angry and afraid. They feared the radioactive contamination of oceans and were furious over what was perceived as an inappropriate American response. The Japanese requested $12–14 million in indemnity payments; $1 million was offered, along with a tepid expression of regret that competed with cynical statements, such as that by one American official who suggested that the fishermen may have been "spying on the tests." The "Lucky Dragon" incident and its aftermath elicited an anti-American bias among ordinary Japanese and a first, belated identification with the suffering of hibakusha. Hibakusha testimonies after "Lucky Dragon" reveal strong anti-nuclear sensibilities.

To capitalize on this public attention, the Casualty Councils and city officials in both Hiroshima and Nagasaki petitioned the national government to pay hibakusha's medical expenses and provide hospital equipment for their care. The national government did provide some money for research purposes, but until 1956 no funds were allocated for medical expenses. Funds raised through the New Year's postal card lotteries were used by the Japanese Red Cross Society to build A-bomb hospitals in Hiroshima (1956) and Nagasaki (1958). In the 1960s other social service institutions opened, including nursing homes and health centers.

Hidankyo, the Japan Confederation of A-bomb and H-bomb Sufferers Organizations, was formed in 1956. In addition to engaging in education and anti-nuclear activism, Hidankyo has lobbied for national relief legislation. Under the provisions of the "Law Concerning Medical Care for A-Bomb Victims," which became effective on April 1, 1957, qualified hibakusha receive free annual physical and laboratory examinations and guaranteed payment for the treatment of illnesses known to be caused by radiation exposure. The law has been revised several times to allow for expanded coverage for affected groups.

Since the 1960s, hibakusha groups and the city governments of Hiroshima and Nagasaki have attempted to obtain passage of an A-bomb Victims Relief Law. Current government aid is classified as "benefits" extended, not "rights" due, but hibakusha have been lobbying for a bill that will recognize their right to be compensated for their war suffering. In 1980 the Ministry of Health and Welfare stated that "a broad standpoint of government compensation does not imply government acknowledgment of its responsibility for any illegal acts on its part."[29]

Responsibility is a major strand of the massive tapestry that is Hiroshima's story. The city's sense of mission is expressed well in the slogan of the Hiroshima International Cultural Foundation, "Hiroshima Belongs to the World." Hiroshima has offered itself to the world as a witness to the effects of nuclear war, a living museum of horror to inspire people to work to insure that nuclear weapons will never be used again.

The stated mission of Hiroshima's public presentation of the bomb — the Peace Memorial Museum, the statues in its Peace Park, the public utterances of its mayors, the fabric of the annual commemoration service — is to be, simply, a warning. Yet the simple passage of time has blurred the sharp awareness that they wish to convey. Hitoshi Motoshima, Nagasaki's current mayor, commented that his counterpart "always wants international conferences to be held in Hiroshima, to gather world executives there. Maybe that's a good thing. But I say, even if Hiroshima and Nagasaki stand on their heads, we haven't preserved one-thousandth of the horror. There's nothing left of the atmosphere, even. So I never talk in those terms."[30]

Hibakusha have tried to encapsulate that horror in voluminous testimony — written and oral accounts, poetry, prose, art, and dance. Social and medical scientists have undertaken an exhaustive documentation of the extent of the atomic bomb disaster, a chilling clinical picture of disease and destruction. Many (perhaps most) hibakusha, though, have chosen to be silent, partly, one suspects, from the frustrating inability to accurately convey the nuances of thought and feeling and the images of destruction wrought by so terrible an event. That task of communication becomes incrementally more difficult for a city, a corporate, public entity, which speaks through pronouncements, mute symbols, and well-crafted images. The public image of Hiroshima has been partially shaped by what one Japanese observer called "professional hibakusha," those who, after many interviews, give stereotyped responses to questions. There is much jealousy in the hibakusha community, long memories about organizational disputes, and decidedly mixed feelings about the large peace groups. Some hibakusha are critical of the press for writing about hibakusha with maudlin sentimentality.

The most serious charge and the one most often leveled against Hiroshima is that it wears the robe of victimhood so securely that the garments of collective responsibility are obscured. A visitor to Hiroshima's Peace Memorial Museum sees little about Japanese militarism, a selective rendering of the past that outrages other Asian leaders. Understandably, Chinese and Koreans are exceptionally sensitive to the way Japan's education ministry portrays the war, a portrayal often characterized by an almost blithe dismissal of responsibility for what is euphemistically referred to as "incidents."

It was not until 1988, when Japan was keeping a death watch for Emperor Hirohito, that the question of wartime responsibility was addressed. Nagasaki Mayor Motoshima became a symbol of rare political courage when he modestly commented, "I think we have been able to reflect sufficiently on the nature of that war.... I think that the Emperor does bear responsibility for the war"[31] and refused to capitulate in the face of right-wing death threats and abandonment by his political allies. (In January 1990 he almost died in an assassination attempt, but recovered to win re-election to a fourth term in 1991.) Over seven thousand people wrote to Mayor Motoshima, praising him for his commitment to free speech, reflecting on their own war experiences, and wrestling with the question of responsibility.

Since these events, Mayor Motoshima has boldly linked the
bomb to the history of Japanese aggression. "The bomb has its
roots in problems going back to the Meiji era. I mean the problems of Japanese aggression, especially the annexation of Korea
in 1910. . . . What we can't lose sight of is that there were people
around the world who rejoiced when the bomb was dropped on
Hiroshima."[32]

The debate over the recent renovation of the Peace Memorial
Hall is indicative of how the potent symbol of Hiroshima is used
by both the right and left. In a debate that was essentially the
same as the dispute over the Smithsonian's planned *Enola Gay*
exhibit, peace groups urged that there be an "aggressor's corner"
that would document the fifteen years of war that proceeded the
bomb. Right-wing groups argued that such exhibits "would be un-
fair to Hiroshima by diluting the uniqueness and eloquence of its
message as a victim of nuclear inferno."[33] The new Peace Memorial Hall, which opened in June 1994, clearly conveys Hiroshima
as a military city that played an important role in Japan's wars
of aggression. It provides factual information on the history of
American development of the bomb, its impact on Hiroshima, and
the course of the nuclear arms race. "The overall effect is to provide a comprehensive *mental* framework for the visitor, who then
goes to the basic display (Museum) for an overwhelming *emotional*
impact."[34]

It is easy to invoke the suffering of hibakusha to present Japan
as the victim of aggression, rather than its perpetrator, and that
is why the work of hibakusha educators has been so important.
Their thoughtful curricula, developed for peace education programs from early grade school to high school graduation, includes
age-appropriate information on the effects of the atomic bombs,
as well as clear documentation of Japanese policies during the
fifteen-year Pacific War.

Some hibakusha have achieved a moral stature that transcends
political ideologies. One of the most eloquent and widely respected
hibakusha leaders was the late Dr. Ichiro Moritaki (1900–1994),
who, at the time of the bombing, was a professor of philosophy
at Hiroshima University. (His teaching career spanned thirty-two
years, 1933–65.) The university was closed during the war, and
Dr. Moritaki supervised mobilized students at Mitsubishi Heavy
Industries, four kilometers from the hypocenter. Dr. Moritaki
would later accuse himself of war crimes for inculcating a nation-
alist ethic in his students, and one of the motivations for his years
of peace activism was a professed need to atone for his wartime
activities.

Dr. Moritaki lost the sight of his right eye when it was pierced by a shard of broken glass; he required several months' hospitalization "for fear that the other eye should also fail and leave me blind. It was during this period that I searched my soul high and low to conceive any prospect for humanity against that inconceivable reality of human calamity in Hiroshima."[35]

Dr. Moritaki came to believe that Hiroshima ushered in, not only the nuclear age, but also a new morality of universalism. That which was "good" before — tribe and nation — is insufficient. What was needed now, he concluded, was an identification with humanity, not with acts of philanthropy, but an actualized knowledge that we are one community with one destiny and our sole loyalty must be to that community. "The system of morality in demand at the present stage of the world history is one that encompasses the entire humanity ... that it should live as a whole. No ethical unit will be valid if it only vindicates the cause of a particular nation."[36] Dr. Moritaki has exemplified these beliefs through his devoted care for individual hibakusha, as an educator, and by the integrity of his many years of leadership in the organized peace movement.

In 1962, in response to international tensions heightened by American and Soviet atmospheric nuclear tests, Dr. Moritaki conceived of a new kind of protest. He sat in silence, in classic Zen posture, in front of the Memorial Cenotaph twenty-four hours a day for twelve days. One day a small child asked him, "Can you abolish nuclear weapons by sitting?" It was, he said, "the great question of my life," and he formulated his response in a phrase he often repeated, that "the chain reaction of spiritual atoms will overcome the chain reaction of material atoms." Eventually other activists joined him in these "sitting protests" — one hour in front of the Cenotaph ("on behalf of the voiceless voices") each time there was a nuclear weapons test. Dr. Moritaki participated in 475 such protests, the last one in July 1993 at the age of ninety-three.

Dr. Moritaki's belief in the chain reaction of spiritual atoms refers to the potential inherent in the post-bomb morality, but at a deeper level it makes reference to Zen teaching about the difficulty of splitting the human ego: a process as laborious and costly as physically splitting the neutron.[37]

Dr. Susumu Ishitani is a Nagasaki hibakusha who was fourteen at the time of the bombing. A third generation Christian, he is a college professor in Tokyo, and as a religious pacifist he has had a long involvement with the Fellowship of Reconciliation. As Christians, the Ishitanis were considered "dangerous and non-patriotic ... loyal to a faith that was different from the state religion." The family decided to remain together in Nagasaki rather than flee the American troops (their encounters with these soldiers were casual but non-stressful.) After the war, Dr. Ishitani's father was diagnosed with tuberculosis and the family moved to Mito where, as a high school student, Susumu Ishitani met Quakers:

> I was shocked and deeply impressed when I met a man from America who said he had been a conscientious objector during the war and came to Japan immediately after the war to help the Japanese people who were in trouble. I had never heard before that there was such a thing as a C.O. existing anywhere in the world. He told us how he got into trouble with his own parents and the community around his family due to his commitment and how he lost one of his kidneys cooperating in a medical experiment in which he was used as a guinea pig.
>
> As I heard him and spent some time with him, I had a firm conviction that this person was showing a real way for Christians to live in the present society. . . . I held a firm conviction that I was a child of God rather than a Japanese, and a human being rather than a member of a nation. . . . I came to have a belief that all human beings are children of God and every man or woman is as precious as anybody else regardless of his or her nationality, sex, color, and social status, and when it is necessary I need to be able to behave like Jesus Christ who lived and died for the benefit of other human beings and for the glory of the Divine.[38]

Susumu Ishitani and his sister barely escaped death because, moments before the explosion, they moved out of the room where they had been; they were, however, exposed to significant amounts of radiation. There was a strong suspicion that their father's tuberculosis, which proved fatal, was exacerbated by radiation, yet Dr. Ishitani never conveys a sense of himself as a victim. Like Dr. Moritaki — and countless hidden, silent hibakusha — he has assumed the burdens of moral leadership and witness.

One Hiroshima activist commented that "people find in Hiroshima what they expect to find." Americans, in particular, look at Hiroshima through a complex prism of emotions, including guilt, anger, shame, discomfort, revenge, and fear. The images of Hiroshima have been mediated to us by government officials, experts, and pro- and anti-nuclear activists who seek to minimize, pathologize, manipulate, defend, or propagandize the experience. It is unfortunate, but not surprising, that most of these commentators have ignored its compelling legacy of human strength and courage.

It is sadly ironic that Hiroshima, a city of silence that contains within itself many kinds of silence, rarely evokes the respectful silence of attentive listening. For many years hibakusha have been telling us their stories but now they are getting older and many are dying. There will come a time when there are no living survivors of Hiroshima and Nagasaki, but before that happens it is incumbent upon us to receive the inheritance of their memories.

2

"I Met the Bomb at . . ."

——— ❦ ———

Hibakusha have presented their testimony in many different ways over the past fifty years as they have tried, in both word and visual imagery, to convey what it was like to have been "under the shadow of the mushroom cloud." Initially constrained by the Occupation-imposed censorship, the first outpouring of hibakusha testimony "came in 1951 when, with the signing of the peace treaty, there was an outburst of public opinion favoring peace and independence. The second peak occurred during the 1954–55 emergence of the movement against nuclear weapons. The third peak came much later, in 1965–71."[1]

Hibakusha testimony is only one portion of the vast body of literature related to the atomic bomb. In addition to the scholarly literature (much of which is inaccessible to the lay person) there are acclaimed works of atomic bomb fiction, such as *Black Rain* (Masuji Ibuse) and *The Devil's Heritage* (Hiroyuki Agawa).[2] Among non-fiction works that approach the eloquence of literature are the memoirs and personal diaries of physicians who experienced the bomb.[3]

Among the earliest volumes of hibakusha testimony were *The Experience of the Atom Bomb*, a 1950 publication by the city of Hiroshima, and *Children of the Atomic Bomb* (October 1951), compiled and edited from over two thousand entries sent to Dr. Arata Osada. The children who had written for the book, elementary, junior, and senior high school students formed the Association of A-Bomb Children in February 1952. Dr. Osada, a professor at Hiroshima University, was an important hibakusha leader until his death in 1961. "I, too, at that time, in a receiving station at the Clothing Depot, was sentenced by the doctors to die, and for four months I roamed in the land of Death before some fate gave me back my life. Since then I have . . . dedicated what is left of my life to a study of 'Education for Peace,' as my offering on behalf of the salvation of mankind."[4] A June 1952 movie, *Children of the Atomic Bomb,* the first film to be made about the aftermath of the bombing, drew on material from the book.

There was an increased output of hibakusha testimony in response to external events (such as the intensification of the U.S.-Soviet arms race) and because of local initiatives. In 1966, the Japanese Broadcasting Corporation (NHK) undertook a project to reconstruct the map of the central bombed area of Hiroshima and issued a public appeal for information about those neighborhoods. Residents responded with such a wealth of personal stories and data that the Hiroshima map reconstruction expanded beyond the central area and a similar effort began in Nagasaki.

At the same time (1964–68) hibakusha, other citizens, peace groups, city officials from Hiroshima and Nagasaki, and prominent writers, historians, and scientists, embarked on a campaign to urge the national government to issue a white paper on the damage caused by the bomb. Toshihiro Kanai, an editorial writer for the *Chugoku Shimbun* proposed a scientifically rigorous, comprehensive survey of bomb damages that would give an accurate indication of the scope of its devastation. Many hoped that such a white paper, disseminated through the United Nations, would serve as a powerful plea for disarmament.

Another important impetus for hibakusha testimony was the 1978–80 "Ten Feet" campaign. In this creative fundraising effort, Japanese citizens were asked to contribute $15 (then 3000 yen), the sum necessary to purchase ten feet of film from the U.S. National Archives. (The entire project, including the production of documentary films, was estimated to cost $400,000.) The film, which had been made in 1946 under the auspices of the U.S. Strategic Bombing Survey, was held in secrecy by the Pentagon until 1976, when it was released to the Archives. Three documentary movies were made from the historical film: *Prophecy, Harvest of Nuclear War,* and *Generation.*[5]

Hirotu Kubouro is representative of those who moved from the ranks of silent hibakusha to an all-consuming activism in conveying his atomic bomb story. Kubouro, nineteen when the bomb was dropped, was exposed two kilometers from the hypocenter while working in the offices of the Japan National Railroad (JNR). He was seriously injured by flying glass, and his physical recovery was hampered by periods of profound depression when he seriously contemplated suicide. Dissuaded only by a sense of responsibility for his widowed father, he decided that he needed to become "a person who could face difficulty," and so presented himself to a Zen monastery for two years of rigorous training. He married, raised a family, continued to work for the railroad, and although he never publicly told his story, in his desire "to console the souls of deceased A-bomb victims," he visited each of the city's more than one hundred memorials to the victims, offering flowers and incense. Eventually he produced a booklet of photographs of the monuments, along with their inscriptions.

In 1977, in preparation for the United Nations First Special Session on Disarmament, he attended a gathering at Hiroshima's YMCA. Impressed by the respect with which the predominantly youthful audience listened to hibakusha and moved by their desire to work for peace, he decided to tell them his story. He is convinced that it is the weight of such narratives that will lead individuals to work against nuclear weapons. His story is not told to elicit sympathy for his pain, but to engender compassion in his listeners. No force, he says, "not even the A-bomb" can "change people's hearts or thinking" except "individuals who understand the distress and pain of others." "I want people to know, to imagine, how people, from babies to old men, suffered and died. I want them to know how so many wanted to, but were unable to help family members. I want them to know the pain, not with their minds, but with their imaginations."[6]

There are volumes of hibakusha testimony untranslated from the Japanese and translations that have failed to find an English-language publisher, personal stories that convey myriad images of the bomb through intimate details. Hibakusha testimony alone cannot teach us about the full dimensions of the bomb, but there is a poignant starkness to these stories that enflesh the statistics of the biologist and historian.

One of the functions of hibakusha testimony is to reclaim the human face from the anonymity of technological warfare, and it is in the small particulars that hibakusha offer of their ordinary daily lives that allow us to identify with their terror. Hibakusha testimony gives us a microscopic rendering of the atomic bomb experience, and although they often say that "only hibakusha can understand hibakusha" they have continually and heroically sought to communicate the details of "a kind of hell on earth."

Japanese is a formulaic language, and that can be seen in the structure of hibakusha testimony. Many begin with a brief description of their general circumstances in August 1945, a detailed narrative of what they saw on the day of the bomb, how they made their escape, the subsequent years of physical and emotional suffering, and the acknowledgment of an event or person or insight that compelled them to act on an inchoate sense of responsibility — to family or history — to narrate their experience. Many ruminate on the question that afflicts all survivors: why did I survive and so many did not? There is an element of random "fate" in almost all these narratives — the fact that a farmer gave them food or drink, a doctor spread oil on a burn, a stranger stopped to pull them from a burning building, the happenstance of being in a different office when the bomb fell or of being sick at home rather than at work in the factory.

There are some hibakusha who have been asked to tell their stories so often that the listener forgets (because their delivery is so polished and smooth) the trauma behind the words, despite the poignant images that are narrated. There are certain images that are repeated because they capsulize the particular horror of the bomb: a dead mother with an infant clasped to her breast, a child crying for a parent, the voice of a woman trapped in a burning building, survivors begging for water, a father mad with grief for the burned child he carries, or the unforgettable sight of hundreds of people walking, "like ghosts," the flesh hanging off their frames.

Other hibakusha speak with such raw emotion that they seem to be physically present to 1945, the rawness a hint that the telling of these stories entails an always painful reliving of their trauma. These narratives are never told for cathartic effect. There is a formalism to hibakusha testimony that serves to balance the horror contained in litanies of frightful images with a necessary restraint that never cheapens the experience with emotionalism.

Dr. Osada offers an eloquent tribute to those who have shared their memories of the bomb:

> When I think of you taking up your pen . . . when I imagine how the remembered figures of those whom you lost came before your eyes, and how you must have talked to them, I feel that these words which you have written are a sort of prayer for the tranquil repose of their souls. If we can publish them, both within our country and without, these words of yours will build in people's hearts an enduring, spiritual Memorial Tower which will surely give joy to the spirits of those who have died. And I believe that not only in Hiroshima, but in all of Japan, and in all the world, people of conscience will offer their hearts' prayers at this Memorial Tower which you have built. Monuments made of stone and bronze may perhaps crumble away after thousands of years. But the A-Bomb Monument which your spirits have built will surely endure forever in the hearts of mankind.[7]

The excerpts that follow, a small but representative sample of hibakusha testimony, are taken from published material, oral history projects, and written statements of speeches. (Statements intended to be spoken are less polished than those prepared for more formal publication, so I have taken the liberty, in some cases, of editing the English translations to make them easier to read.) Most of the people represented in this section are non-activist hibakusha, with the exception of the Hiroshima poet Sadako Kurihara and the Nagasaki physician Tatsuichiro Akizuki, M.D. If known, I have included the author's distance from the hypocenter and his or her age in August 1945.

Hibakusha testimony in English often includes the evocative phrase, "I met the bomb at . . ." These are some memories of "that day."

Sadako Ueno experienced the bomb in Hiroshima:

Whirling, the whole grew into a mushroom shape, and at 10,000 feet it merged into a mass of summer cloud.

Beneath this, all was silence and darkness. This may have lasted five or six minutes, or perhaps only thirty seconds: horrible, dead black silence! It was broken by the sudden cries and groans of injured people. Slowly the light came back and we could hear the screaming of people pinned down by the fallen walls, flying glass and debris. . . .

At Hatchobori, from under a fallen house I saw a left hand and wrist protruding, and heard, "Help me, help me," but I could not stop. I ran on, thinking of nothing but getting to safety. Suddenly I came out on the river bank, where thousands of wounded people were crowded. At the bridge, refugees were trying to climb onto fishing boats to sail upriver to a safer place, but those already on board pushed them off to keep the boats from sinking. . . .

Over a period of ten years, forty pieces of glass have been removed from my body, but those remaining seem to be a part of me now. My white corpuscle count fluctuates by 10,000, but there will probably be no sudden change. On my left elbow there is an ugly scar, but thankfully, it is not like a keloid, which aches with the changing seasons. However, I carry keloids over the scars in my heart, much, much worse than those on the arm.[8]

Masao Kayo was two kilometers from the hypocenter in Hiroshima:

Right after the flash I was blown away and fainted. Screams of girls I heard then still haunt me to this day. I had cuts and burns all over my body and I couldn't use my left eye. With the help of a young soldier, I was wandering around Hiroshima's sea of fire. Grief of leaving injured people behind in the fire, the sight of a severely burned mother with her baby on her back, tottering, people ran crazily, screaming, bodies left on both sides of the streets, people crying over them, all the things I saw. And I felt the hopelessness that I can't do anything for them. Could this cruelty exist? This is hell. Again, I fainted on a river bank. I recovered consciousness to find myself wet with blood and rain. I couldn't stop shivering from a high fever. Since there was no medicine and water, I thought I would die. At a Buddhist temple where I was taken to, I suffered from immense pain without drinking water and food for three days. People cried their mothers' and families' names and died one after another without drinking water.[9]

Hiroshi Sawachika, M.D., was a twenty-seven-year-old army surgeon stationed in Hiroshima and was exposed to the bomb 4.7 kilometers from the hypocenter:

. . . a strange group of wailing survivors approached the first aid station. On closer inspection I noted that it was a group of badly burnt survivors with their clothes torn to shreds. . . . We were overwhelmed by this large group of survivors with burns, but we immediately made available a large hall for them. Having no burn ointment, we obtained a drum of peanut oil from the warehouse and mixed it with talc and prepared ointment to treat their burns. Soldiers also took part in emergency treatment. The strange odor of this mixture of peanut oil and talc which soon filled the hall reminded me of dried cuttlefish fried in cooking oil. The number of survivors increased, some of whom had undergone treatment but many were waiting to be treated. The number increased and the long building along the bay was transformed into an emergency field hospital. The number of survivors lying prostrate on the ground increased endlessly.[10]

The next four entries are taken from narratives accompanying drawings that were collected by the Japanese Broadcasting Corporation (NHK) in 1974. In May 1974 a seventy-seven-year-old hibakusha came to the television studio with a picture he had drawn based on his memories of the bomb. Awed by its visual power, the station issued an appeal, "Let us Leave for Posterity Pictures about the Atom-Bomb Drawn by Citizens." Between June and August 1974 they received 975 drawings and paintings by hibakusha, none of whom were professional artists. Many of the drawings were accompanied by evocative descriptions.

Mikio Inoue was thirty-eight when he was exposed to the bomb in Hiroshima:

We were on our way home. We were walking along the streetcar line at the foot of Hijiyama. Wherever we went we saw dead horses and bodies lying here and there. The remaining fires were giving off a lot of smoke. Not a soul was in sight. It was when I crossed Miyuki Bridge that I saw Professor Takenaka standing at the foot of the bridge. . . . He was almost naked, wearing nothing but shorts, and he had a rice ball in his right hand. Beyond the streetcar line, the northern area was covered by red fire burning against the sky. Far away from the line, Ote-machi was also a sea of fire.

That day Professor Takenaka had not gone to Hiroshima University and the A-bomb exploded when he was at home. He tried to rescue his wife who was trapped under a roofbeam but all his efforts were in vain. The fire was threatening him also. His wife pleaded, "Run away, dear!" He was forced to desert his wife and escape from the fire. He was now at the foot of Miyuki Bridge.

But I wonder how he came to hold that rice ball in his hand? His naked figure, standing there before the flames with that rice ball looked to me as symbol of the modest hopes of human beings.[11]

Kinzo Nishida was exposed to the bomb in Hiroshima when he was forty-eight years old:

It was about 9:30 A.M., August 6, 1945. While taking my severely wounded wife out to the riverbank by the side of the hill of Nakahiromachi, I was horrified, indeed, at the sight of a stark naked man standing in the rain with his eyeball in his palm. He looked to be in great pain but there was nothing that I could do for him.

I wonder what became of him. Even today, I vividly remember the sight. It was simply miserable.[12]

Hiroshima resident Suemi Kajiya was thirty-five in 1945:

The mother's entire back was burned but her front was not injured. Her breasts, especially, appeared normal so that her baby was clinging to them to suckle. The baby was strong and moved from his mother's breasts to the ground and back again. I guessed that she had lain face down with her baby under her body because her front side and her baby remained unburned. She was unconscious. I was afraid she would die soon and the baby's milk would be stopped.[13]

Akiko Takakura experienced the Hiroshima bombing at age seventeen:

The corpse lying on its back on the road had been killed immediately when the A-bomb was dropped. Its hand was lifted to the sky and the fingers were burning with blue flames. The fingers were shortened to one-third and distorted. A dark liquid was running to the ground along the hand. This hand must have embraced a child before.[14]

Yoshiko Motoyasu experienced the bomb in Hiroshima at age fourteen:

When I awoke, it was morning, and I was finally able to tell my name and address to an officer. For two days I alternately fainted and awoke, but on August 8th, a neighbor found me and called my mother. She took me to a doctor, who cut open my swollen hand without anesthetic, and found maggots crawling about. The pain of having them cleaned out I shall never forget. After the hand, the doctor treated wounds on my other hand, my face, my shoulder and my legs. I screamed so loudly and so long that my voice failed. For half a year I could not stand, or even move my body.

Now, surrounded by my children, an ordinary mother and worker for the telephone office, with many friends, I still have half my face covered with keloids. These are the wounds of hate.[15]

Tameko Fukuda was repatriated from Korea in September 1945 and returned to Hiroshima:

About a week later I met a stranger who said, "What are you doing?" We were just wandering around in the burned-out remains. So I said, "My mother was no doubt killed by the bomb, and I am looking around for the remains of her body." "Oh," she said, "if it was Grandma Fukuda she fell down near the entrance over there." She took me to the place saying, "Our house was located there so grandmother's house was here."

So my children and I used shovels to dig around and we found her. How did we know for sure? Grandma was color blind and she wore blue-colored clothes all the time. Since we knew this, when we saw the piece of cloth we said, "Oh, that blue kimono was Grandma's. That body must be hers." The body was just at the entrance. We had to dig out her bones and then bring them back. We brought her bones back to the family home and had a memorial service. But to say that is somewhat of an overstatement. There was no Buddhist temple or priest around. "What shall we do?" My oldest girl said, "Mother, one of my friends is a Buddhist priest's daughter. Why don't I ask her?" So we brought the bones and in the burned-out city the Buddhist priest had built a little shack.[16]

Hiroko Harada was five years old in 1945. She, her mother, and two young siblings had been evacuated to the country and were living with her grandmother. Her father and elder sister remained in Hiroshima:

My father wasn't hurt at all but my sister was very badly hurt. Since my sister was working with the Labor Group that was clearing away the houses at Tsurumi Bridge, from her face to her feet her whole body was very badly burned. For a while they said she couldn't be saved and Mother was crying. But now she is all right.

However, her face and her body are all covered with scars and she still can't use her left hand very well. She had two operations on her hand but it still isn't fixed. When it gets to be autumn and winter, since the skin of her hands and legs and all the places where she was burned is thin, her skin splits and she is in an awfully bad way. Every now and then an automobile comes for her from the Occupation Army and they take her for an examination. But no matter how many times she goes, they just look at her and don't give her any treatment.

And my sister always complains, "It's so stupid!"

My mother is always worrying and looking sad because she's afraid that with all those burns my sister won't be able to find anyone to marry her.[17]

Itsuo Kojima experienced the atomic bomb in Hiroshima:

Flames covered everything. It was Hell. People cried everywhere for water but no one paid any attention, and so they died, one by one, before my eyes. In their suffering, many jumped into the river until the current was dammed with the bodies of groaning people lying in the bloody mud. No director, no matter how skilled, could produce a film to equal this miserable sequence.

I hate war! Surely one who has suffered to the point of death cannot exist without crying out, "I hate war!"

Then why is it that people are not shouting this aloud? It is because our government's policy is to discourage people from concerning themselves with problems of peace. The mass media, controlled by government, carry out this policy.

But man must live! In order to live in peace, we must have courage and wisdom![18]

Hitoshi Takayama experienced the bomb in Hiroshima:

I walked back to Hiroshima along the bus route. Military people, civilians, injured people — all of them were completely silent — just struggled along the road. The fighting spirit of everyone was completely gone. . . . Victims were lying down everywhere in the open spaces. Small voices called for water and there were many dead. They had been in the hot summer sun for three days. The scene was terrible, but the smell was worse. When I got to the bottom of the mountain I was feeling very sick. At last I got to the streetcar line and the fallen telephone poles were still smoking. Burned, black people had fallen down along the street. Nearby a burned man was holding a badly burned child to his breast. He asked me to help him bring the child into the shade and put him on a mat. I did. I shall never forget the mixture of the feelings of the father's love for his child and the pitiful condition they were in. This scene is etched on my heart.[19]

Tatsuichiro Akizuki, M.D., was twenty-nine years old in 1945. A physician working at a small tuberculosis hospital in Nagasaki, he was in the middle of an operation when the bomb fell:

The defeat and surrender of Japan, the end of the war, caused no excitement in Urakami and Nagasaki, which had been in ruins since August 9. There was hardly anyone there to get excited, and nothing to be excited about: there was no object which had not been scorched or destroyed, no person who had escaped injury or death. We now heard more about the important broadcast [of the emperor].

[Dr. Akizuki read the emperor's statement to the patients in his hospital:]

It was all too late. As I read on, I wanted to ask why our leaders had found it necessary to call down such misery on us in the furtherance of what they called a sacred war? . . .

I read through the statement with frequent pauses. Most of the others were weeping silently, the nurses were sobbing aloud. At the end I murmured dejectedly: "You lost your families and your homes when the atomic bomb exploded — now you have lost your country."

But at the same time, this realization that we had lost everything seemed to take a load off my mind. For now we had nothing left to lose.[20]

Tokihiko Shimizu experienced the atomic bomb in Nagasaki:

In the remains of the burned city, every night and every day, from here and there, from school grounds and other places, smoke rose from cremated bodies. That stench continued for days and days. When evening came the smell was even stronger. Under the atomic bomb cloud, many of my friends were blasted and burned to death.

When I went to give my condolences to parents of friends who had died, their parents looked at me as if to say, "Why are you still alive?" I can never forget the look in their eyes.[21]

Hiroshima resident Sizue Hotta was a nurse in Hiroshima. She was ten kilometers from the hypocenter when the bomb fell:

I believe it is my duty as a hibakusha to tell the truth of Hiroshima to the world's people. In America and Europe most people don't know how cruelly and seriously the radioactivity of the atomic bomb afflicted numberless citizens. Their understanding of nuclear weapons is only about its enormous destructive power and intense heat. It was not made known that nuclear weapons emitted radiation. They think that they will be safe if they are distant from the hypocenter, and are easily taken prisoner by the so-called "nuclear deterrent theory."[22]

Kayako Nakanishi experienced the bomb in Hiroshima:

At the hospital I receive treatment — but there is no name for my sickness....

Second-generation victims — now in their thirties and forties — who were born at that time are getting regular examinations. But there is a big problem of marriage for victims. From old times if there was something wrong with the girl to be married, the marriage would be impossible. In my case, too, because I got ill my mother-in-law said that I, as an atomic bomb victim, was like a huge debt. I felt very sad when I heard her say that. Second generation victims are also having much trouble in finding mates. In the third generation this problem will no doubt continue.

In this way we are forced to live on in a hell-like, despairing condition.[23]

Setsuko Yamamoto, Hiroshima, was in the first grade in 1945:

...thanks to my two parents, I who had been sickly became so healthy that you would hardly know me. And I am living happily. However on account of the A-bomb burns, the little finger of my right hand is all twisted and sometimes when the bad boys say mean things and tease me, I get mad.

Every day in the trolleys and as I'm walking along the streets, whenever I see people with big scars from burns on their faces and necks and hands and so on, I think that practically all of them are from wounds they got at the time of the A-bomb and I have a feeling that I would like to run up to them so we could comfort and encourage each other. I believe that this is a common spirit among all the survivors. Those of us who have actually experienced with our bodies the fact that war is a frightful and wretched business — we earnestly wish to do everything in our power to be friendly with all the people of the world and to make peace last forever.[24]

Kozo Itagaki was 1.8 kilometers from the hypocenter of the Hiroshima bomb:

An evening-like darkness due to soot and smoke from fires broke out here and there. Victims of the blast seemed like ghosts, without a vestige of clothing on their sore and burned bodies and it was hard to distinguish their sex if you didn't take a close look. They were tottering toward the park, avoiding persons who had sunk to the ground. They were asking for help and water in a faint voice, with their arms held out, and with the skin peeled and hung down like potato skins. Supposedly they thought there must be some remedy if they could reach the top of the hill. But the next morning those who finally reached the top were dead, falling one upon another without being able to get medical treatment. Together with some relatively healthy soldiers I spent days relieving injured persons in the city, collecting corpses, burying or incinerating them, putting ashes in order, and so on. At around noon about four days after the incident, when we were at rest, a boy (he looked like a third grader) came up with tottering steps and said, "Soldier, please give me water." I looked at him and saw that the boy had a sign of jaundice. He also showed signs of dehydration. His hair had partly fallen out. Everyone who happened to be there agreed that if he drank water he would die. I said I would bring him some a little later, and told him to lie down under the tree for a while. And we proceeded with our conversation. Suddenly I noticed the boy drinking sewage with his head down deep in the gutter nearby. Soon he died.

Now I am a parent of a child and whenever I recall the happenings I imagine how hard the boy was crying for Father and Mother in his heart, or if the parents had been on the spot how much they would have felt frantic; and I regret that I didn't let him drink water there and then.[25]

Thomas Takeshita was eight hundred meters from the hypocenter in Hiroshima:

I was placed in a hospital, but the hospital was closed soon after-ward. It is impossible to describe in words my sufferings during the fifty-two hours before I finally was reunited with my family in Kagoshima Prefecture. I was hounded by the hibakusha symptoms from the time I returned to the university until I graduated, and I always lamented my hapless fate.

However, I experienced a strange feeling two years ago in Geth-semane on holy Mt. Olive in Jerusalem. It was the consciousness that my being in Hiroshima on that historic day was not bad luck, but God giving me a special responsibility. . . .

This is because I am convinced that my experience is an ex-perience of the century and is worth appealing to the whole world.[26]

Shigeru Tasaka was a third-grade student in Hiroshima in 1945:

When the end of the war came everyone was weeping with disap-pointment. I also was very sad but in other ways I was relieved. I think it would have been a good thing if, in the course of this war, atom bombs had fallen on every country and the people of all those countries had experienced the atom bomb. This is because I believe that by experiencing atom bombs people will understand how bar-baric, how tragic, how uncivilized, how hateful a thing war is, and we could have an end of the revolting wars that we have now.[27]

Masahito Hirose, a Nagasaki hibakusha, was fifteen at the time of the bomb. He was 4.5 kilometers from the hypocenter:

My cousin, who lived with my family, was working in a small fac-tory near the hypocenter then. That morning I left with him and parted from him on the way. We went in opposite directions. He was burnt by the heat-ray beyond imagination and disappeared. He left nothing behind, not even a piece of bone.

As he did not come home that night, my aunt, his mother, went out to look for him the next morning. It was in vain. But she went out the next morning and the next. She came home exhausted every evening. On the seventh day she could not get up from her bed. She ran a high fever. Her gums bled. The bleeding would not stop. Her hair came off in a cluster. She died calling her son's name. Her death was because of the radiation effect of the A-bombing. So many people who had never been injured and burnt fell down to die one after another. We did not know that it was because of the radiation effect.[28]

Issaki Takeuchi was a soldier assigned to Hiroshima's First Army Hospital:

When we went south for about thirty minutes, it began to rain suddenly. It was gummy and black, for it contained the atomic ashes, which was ascertained later. The pouring rain pierced my burnt skin and I felt very chilly though it was midsummer in August. It kept on raining for more than three or four hours, I remember.

We got to the headquarters of the hospital. The barracks were burning from both ends. I heard many faint voices calling for help . . . soldiers pressed under the crushed barracks. We soon made desperate efforts to rescue them, but there was no way we could do it with only a few men. The voices were still heard continuously, but our efforts ended in vain.[29]

Fumi Itoh experienced the bomb in Hiroshima:

Often during that time we got word of a schoolgirl who had the same name and age, and rushed off with hearts leaping for joy at the prospect of seeing our daughter once again . . . but all in vain as we found ourselves making wild goose chases after girls who had nothing in common with our daughter. Taking our lunches, we would set out expectantly first thing in the morning for various evacuation points, thinking, "Today's the day!" only to return after dark, dragging our feet wearily, our tears flowing unrestrained.

Then after a week, news of the circumstances of our daughter's death was brought by a friend who had fled the city at the time and later returned, and thus finally was cut the last slender thread of our hope. [Their daughter had been pinned under the ruins of her school and burned to death.]

. . . That same friend who gave us this news, even though he had received only a slight burn, and appeared on the surface to have suffered no serious injury, developed symptoms of atomic bomb radiation sickness a month later, and died writhing in agony. When I heard this, I was overwhelmed by an indescribable feeling of pity. I should at least be glad that my own child's suffering had been brief. . . .

Every time I catch sight of young girls, whose disfigured faces tell you from a single glance that they bear the scars of the atomic bomb, I try to imagine what it must feel like for these people who must go on living looking the way they do. Those with perma-

nent scars no doubt feel a sense of isolation, and yet, I suppose are resigned to their lot.

Then, when I think of a student who played truant that day and went off to play with two of her friends, and thereby survived uninjured, and hear that both she and her parents speak of it with an air of smugness, I get an unspeakably wretched feeling, and my mind becomes a chaos of conflicting thoughts. . . .

Who in the world was it that kept promoting the war, driving a young girl of only sixteen to obey government directives unquestioningly and, giving up all thought of her own pleasure, simply to sacrifice her entire youth for the sake of our country's victory? Who caused her to abandon her judgment of right and wrong for a naive, one-track way of life, depriving her of adequate food and clothing each day in that never-ending war? Who should bear the responsibility for promoting the war effort with slogans of "student mobilization" and "labor service," and, in the end, for robbing her of her very life? I almost went out of my mind with indignation at the thought of it all.[30]

Hisae Aoki experienced the bomb in Nagasaki at age eighteen:

Army personnel were busy treating the wounded at the school. I had my wounds disinfected and was placed in a large, broken-down classroom. The two men who had carried me brought a bed quilt from somewhere and spoke to me with great kindness. I could only shed tears of gratitude. I asked their names repeatedly and finally they gave me their name cards. I started in surprise when I saw the cards. They were Korean. I was ignored by my own fellow Japanese but two people from a foreign country had rescued me. I thanked them with all my heart. I later lost the name cards and so now there is no way for me to express my gratitude to them, wherever they are.[31]

Masako Yoshinaga was fourteen when she experienced the Nagasaki bomb:

My hair fell out, and my gums began to bleed. Severe recurring diarrhea made me feeble and skinny. The roots of my nails became purulent, and the purulent infection in my right foot became so bad that the bones were exposed.

Radiation sickness did not just kill the badly wounded. . . . I was much afraid that I might die next. I did not die, but for the next ten years I had to struggle against illness aggravated by radiation disease. I was hospitalized over and over again, first for appendicitis, then for peritonitis, pleurisy, tuberculosis and the like. My ado-

lescence was miserable: I couldn't get a job; I couldn't get health insurance benefits; I could not pay for my hospitalization. Worse still, I had developed ugly keloid tumors. How I envied young girls in their miniskirts and bathing suits!

Fortunately I was able to marry, but I was still very feeble. I was anxious about my coming baby: I felt as if I were carrying a time-bomb inside myself.

Now it is my great pleasure that my three children have grown up without any big problems.[32]

Tsukasa Uchida experienced the atomic bomb in Nagasaki:

My mother and I had lost all means of support in the midst of the post-war confusion, and we had to endure the cold, lonely winter outdoors. She got up at 4:30 every morning, bought whole cart-loads of vegetables from farmers carrying them into the city, and then sold the vegetables wholesale.... Among the small retail dealers in the market was an old handicapped woman who had no living relatives. She had been hit by a truck driven by the Occupation forces and she was partially paralyzed from the waist down. Nobody offered her a healing hand, though, no doubt because we were so hardened by the austerity of our own lives.

After the summer of 1946, makeshift huts were erected.... We built a house on our property, and a few days after it was completed the old woman mentioned above appeared at the doorstep with a mat and asked if she could sleep on the earthen floor of the entranceway. At first we let her sleep on the earthen floor, but it was a pathetic sight and so we gave her a place on the boarded upper floor. When winter came around her hands and feet became red and chapped with frostbite.

One day the old woman gathered charcoal from the ruins and brought it into the house to make a fire. Looking at it more closely, I was astonished to find among it the charred fragments of human bones. We were literally living in a graveyard. My mother said that it was some kind of message and she looked after the old woman until the very end of her life.[33]

Noriko Hanayama, seventeen years old in 1945, was one kilometer from the hypocenter in Nagasaki:

After graduating from a girls' high school, I became a teacher. I was often called "Hage" (a baldhead) because of my thin hair. Being embarrassed, I wore a cap for about four years. In 1957, I had to give up teaching because of the aftereffects of A-bomb radiation. In addition to that, being an A-bomb victim was also an obstacle *to marriage, but fortunately, I did get married and gave birth to three children. My second child was deformed and died immediately after birth. Why should even the child of an A-bomb victim suffer this fate? I spent my time in tears.*[34]

Nuiko Sugito, a Nagasaki hibakusha, was twenty-two at the time of the bombing. She was four kilometers from the hypocenter:

I have never forgotten the horrible experience of the atomic bomb. It is still fresh in my memory. However, for fear of discrimination against the survivors and their children, I hesitated to apply for a special certificate for atomic bomb victims. I wanted to stay away from the issue rather than expose myself as a survivor.

After I had raised my four children, I made up my mind to get involved in a peace movement. . . . I am getting old and so are the other survivors, but it is our duty to hand down our experience from generation to generation. I just keep going as long as I live.[35]

Yoshinori Yokokawa was sixteen when he experienced the Hiroshima bomb. The incident referred to in this narrative took place in April 1949, at which time he was teaching at Niho Primary School, four kilometers from the hypocenter:

One day, a child playing in the mud shouted, "Sir. Here is something strange. What is it?" When I reached him, there were already many children gathering there, noisily digging in the ground.

Those white things, evidently bones, came jangling out one after another. Children shouted here and there, "Sir, here is another." The pupils in their first school year could not know that they were fragments of bones. Appalled, I kept standing there with the bones handed to me by a child, without telling them to stop digging up the ground. . . . The weathered bones were fragile, reminding me of that August 6, 1945.[36]

Hisashi Aoki was 2.8 kilometers from the Nagasaki hypocenter:

When the war ended, though, I went back to Nagasaki. The city had changed to a barren field of rubble, and Michino'o Station bustled with people going in search of relatives or fleeing to the country in fear of the American occupation. Rumors had spread that the first thing to be requisitioned by the American soldiers would be women, and then cows and goats for food. Because of this there were abandoned cows and goats wandering about the streets.[37]

Sadako Kurihara was thirty-two when she experienced
the Hiroshima bomb:

[Sadako Kurihara, one of Hiroshima's most acclaimed poets, is also
respected for her inveterate anti-nuclear activism. Her work as editor of the magazine *Chugoku Bunka* (Chugoku Culture) brought
her and her husband into conflict with Occupation censors. One of
her most famous poems is "We Shall Bring Forth New Life."]

It was night in the basement of a broken building.
Victims of the atomic bomb
Crowded into the candleless darkness,
Filling the room to overflowing —
The smell of fresh blood, the stench of death,
The stuffiness of human sweat, the writhing moans —
When, out of the darkness, came a wondrous voice.
"Oh! The baby's coming!" it said.
In the basement turned to living hell
A young woman had gone into labor!
The others forgot their own pain in their concern:
What could they do for her, having not even a match
To bring light to the darkness?
Then came another voice: "I am a midwife.
I can help her with the baby."
It was a woman who had been moaning in pain only mo-
   ments before.
And so, a new life was born
In the darkness of that living hell.
And so, the midwife died before the dawn,
Still soaked in the blood of her own wounds.
We shall give forth new life!
We shall bring forth new life!
Even to our death.[38]

I wrote this poem at the end of the horrific month of August, at
a time when corpses lay everywhere in Hiroshima. And the people
who were not suffering from the direct effects of the bombardment
were slowly dying from the effects of the radiation. At a time like
this, new life had been born; I was fascinated, and had to write it
down. What does this birth, this new life, in that dark cellar mean?
It was the birth of a new Hiroshima, a Hiroshima that would not
cease to long for peace in the world. It happened at the end of
a fifteen-year expansionist war waged by Japanese imperialism in
Asia. What does this blood-covered midwife mean who died before
she could see the dawn? She is a symbol of those 200,000 people
killed by the bomb, who died without experiencing the first day

of peace, August 15. *Difficult though it may be, we must bring up Hiroshima and create a world of peace in which there are neither atomic weapons nor wars.*[39]

Tatsuichiro Akizuki, M.D.:

People often say in Japan: "Kamikaze, the divine wind, will blow."

Kamikaze was the historic typhoon which, when the Mongols invaded our islands, blew and destroyed the enemy.... The typhoon after the atomic bomb attacks was our Kamikaze, which saved the people from secondary effects of radioactive fall-out. [There were heavy rains in Nagasaki on September 2–3, 1945.]

After the typhoon, the death toll suddenly decreased near the hospital; the advancing tide of death retreated and sank like water into the ground. The staff and I recovered from our feelings of nausea, from the symptoms of radiation sickness.

From that day on, the apparent inevitability of death was transformed into a reassertion of life. We did not know why this should be so, but the daily fear that we would all soon die, gradually diminished as, day by day, autumn turned into winter and the year came to an end.

The dead were dead; but those who survived could start to live once more.[40]

3

The Symbolic American

BARBARA REYNOLDS

I'll never forget one evening when I was walking to the Friendship Center, and I saw a woman coming toward me leading somebody. This person had a huge, swollen head. It looked like a cauliflower ...the face was not recognizable. It was just the most horrible looking face. When they saw me coming they went over and stood in the shadows; the person turned its head toward the wall until I went by. When I got to the Center, I told a woman there about it and she said, "A lot of them don't go out until after dark. Then they are taken for a walk, and go back to their rooms."[1]

— *Barbara Reynolds*

In 1975, Barbara Reynolds was given honorary citizenship in Hiroshima, an official recognition of her deep attachment to the city she had first come to twenty-four years earlier.[2] In 1951 the Reynolds family (Barbara, her husband Earle, and their three children) moved to Japan when Earle, a physical anthropologist, accepted a research position at the Hiroshima branch of the Atomic Bomb Casualty Commission (ABCC). They lived on a nearby military base, but outside of Earle's work, the family had only minimal contact with hibakusha. It would take ten years, and eventful inner and outer journeys, before Barbara's ignorance and apathy were transformed into a passionate involvement with hibakusha.

There are many dimensions to Barbara Reynolds's story. At the simplest level it is the story of a personal transformation from political apathy to activism, of one woman's willingness to be open to, and respond to, the suffering of hibakusha. Barbara's most intensive involvement with hibakusha occurred, roughly, during a twenty-year period (1958 to 1978) that coincided with major changes in the hibakusha community. The constraints of the Occupation had ended — the artificial silence imposed by the Press

Code, the combination of anger and subservience that marked their dealings with official institutions like ABCC — and hibakusha had begun to articulate a sophisticated anti-nuclear message, concomitant with a clear insistence on their right to medical and financial compensation instead of charitable kindness. One result of this transformation from helpless victims to responsible actors was a change in their relationship with Americans.

Hibakusha sought out people who shared a commitment to work for the abolition of nuclear weapons, and they accepted Barbara as one of their allies. The peace pilgrimage was Barbara's contribution to Hiroshima's repertoire, and she always thought it significant that its format evolved, not from political discussion, but from a day of prayer and fasting in the Peace Park. In later years, as her personal and public relationship with hibakusha became more demanding, Barbara would think of that first peace pilgrimage as being naively optimistic. If it appears that way in retrospect it also reflects the core beliefs that informed all of her work: that individually and as a people we had to acknowledge responsibility for the bomb, and the only way we could do that was through an engagement with hibakusha.

The World Friendship Center is the most visible of Barbara's legacies in Hiroshima. She envisioned the Center as a place of dialogue, where hibakusha and Japanese and international visitors could come together to learn about the atomic bomb and explore ways of strengthening Hiroshima's nascent spirit of internationalism. The ethos of the Friendship Center is imbued with a quintessential American idealism — Barbara's inheritance from her middle-class, mid-American childhood — but there was a more direct influence from the beliefs Barbara adopted after her 1964 conversion experience. She always narrated the story of that conversion (from tepid religiosity to passionate faith) with delicate restraint (her response drawn in shadow so as to attract the viewer's attention to the light of God's action). It was all the more powerful because it came in the aftermath of a shattering divorce (ending a twenty-nine-year marriage), amid a time of financial insecurity and social isolation.

Those losses led her first to God and then to a closer, more empathetic identification with hibakusha ("experts by virtue of their suffering"). She spoke of her desire to be "a symbol of the power of Jesus — not as an American, but as a Christian," and she sought to find actions to express a need to atone for the use of the bomb. Ironically, when she became a symbol, it was as an American, and she could not control how people responded to her; some Japanese used her as a foil for their anger, while others acted toward her out of a desire for reconciliation. Barbara had to negotiate a complex relationship with hibakusha, walking a path that had previously been untrod, and despite her difficulties and losses, her loneliness and confusion, she remained intrepidly faithful to her unique vocation.

Barbara's public life in Hiroshima began in 1960, and her subsequent peace work drew on a reservoir of good will generated by those Americans who, during the previous decade, had begun the work of reconciliation; many were religious pacifists whose opposition to nuclear weapons included charitable efforts on behalf of hibakusha.

These early witnesses are relatively unknown in this country, and included people like Floyd Schmoe, a Quaker professor of dendrology at the University of Washington. Dr. Schmoe, who had assisted Japanese Americans incarcerated in the relocation camps in the United States during the war, privately raised funds, and in the summers from 1949 through 1951, he went to Hiroshima with wood, carpentry tools, and a group of international volunteers (which always included Korean students) and eventually built a total of nineteen much-needed homes for hibakusha.

Norman Cousins also made his first visit to Hiroshima in 1949. Then editor of the *Saturday Review,* in whose pages he had condemned the use of the bomb, Cousins organized a "Moral Adoption Movement" whereby Americans could provide financial support for children orphaned by the bomb; eventually over five hundred orphans were assisted by this program. Cousins also played an instrumental role in the 1955–56 Hiroshima Maidens project, conceived by the Hiroshima Protestant pastor Rev. Kiyoshi Tanimoto (one of the six hibakusha whose stories were told in John Hersey's *Hiroshima*). Twenty-five young women hibakusha received multiple plastic surgeries at New York's Mt. Sinai Hospital and recuperated, emotionally as well as physically, in the homes of Quakers in suburban New York. One hundred and thirty-eight separate surgeries were performed on their disfiguring, crippling keloid scars.[3]

In 1957 two American writers, Edita and Ira Morris, opened Hiroshima House, a project subsequently supported by the Japan chapter of P.E.N. The House ran recreational programs and provided lodging for hibakusha who had to travel to Hiroshima for medical treatment at the Atomic Bomb Hospital.[4]

For a brief period of time — largely due to the popularity of John Hersey's *Hiroshima* — American press reports about the bomb described not only its awesome power but the depth of suffering it caused, rescuing hibakusha from the anonymity imposed by technological warfare. Projects like the Hiroshima Maidens and the Moral Adoption Movement not only provided needed assistance to hibakusha, but they allowed individual Americans to respond to individual hibakusha. In a 1985 speech, on the occasion of being honored by the War Resisters League, Barbara Reynolds remarked that hibakusha "feel sorry for us because we carry the burden of the conscience from the bombing." Yet, in trying to ameliorate that burden by acts of charity and good will, Americans elicited complex feelings of resentment and dependency in hibakusha.[5]

Arguably the person who had the greatest impact on mediating American concern for hibakusha during those early years was Mary McMillan (1912–91), a long-term Methodist missionary who went on to serve as president of Hiroshima's Jogakuin Women's College. McMillan had been in Japan a mere eighteen months before the war began, and she was forced to return to the United States. She continued her Japanese studies at Berkeley, and then taught Nisei students interred in a relocation camp in Utah. She was the first American missionary invited back to Japan (in January 1947) and the "railroad station speech" she gave upon her return has attained the status of a Hiroshima legend.[6]

A colleague, Doris Hartman, remembered McMillan's reflections on that speech. "As soon as I got to Hiroshima, I apologized for what my government had done. I told them our government has two sides, the one that wants to do good, and yet, sometimes we get all worked up and do horrible things." Hartman continues: "This apology had a powerful effect on many who heard it, and she was able to found a chapter of the Fellowship of Reconciliation (FOR) as well as help with a panel of peacemaking that included the city mayor."[7] McMillan recalled FOR meetings during the Occupation:

> At the time, these meetings were a frustrating burden because I was always forced into the position of chairman by the absence of any other Christian among the many kinds of Japanese who gathered, attracted by, but not yet grounded in, Christian pacifist teachings. Those attending these study-fellowship sessions always included victims of the bomb. The turn-over was so great that the group seemed to remain on the kindergarten level, always recapitulating and interpreting for newcomers the ABCs of Christian pacifism, while some members' primary interest in the meeting seemed to be, for lack of a better term, "group therapy" for bereaved friends whom they brought. Looking back now, perhaps it can be said that those occasions were God-given opportunities for those members who were not victims or survivors to learn the plight and hopes of these people, as well as to plant the seeds

of teachings of non-violence, and to recognize one another as mutual cross-bearers in that particular situation.[8]

The Voyage of the *Phoenix*

Mary McMillan, Floyd Schmoe, and Norman Cousins came to Hiroshima and acted as they did out of mature political and religious commitments. In contrast, Barbara Reynolds was apolitical when she arrived in Hiroshima, content in her roles of wife and mother, choices that were consistent with her own happy childhood. This was the legacy of parents who "loved each other and believed that marriage was for keeps, and who brought up their only child in the assurance that it is an exciting privilege to be a woman — but one that carries responsibilities... for nurturance and servanthood and sacrifice."[9] Her mother, who had retired from teaching to raise Barbara, maintained an interest in child development through a part-time career in testing and critiquing playthings. Her father, a college English professor and poet, drowned in a boating accident when Barbara was fifteen. It was a devastating loss, and before it was "fully accepted and resolved," Barbara married Earle Reynolds, then a doctoral student in anthropology. They would become the parents of two sons, Tim and Ted, and a daughter, Jessica.

Like her mother, Barbara combined domestic responsibilities with an at-home career; she was the published author of six children's books, several of which had Japanese themes. Barbara attributed her deep affection for Japan to a childhood book, *The Japanese Twins*. So abiding was that affection that she was inoculated even against the virulence of wartime propaganda. "I hated what the war was doing, hated the killing on both sides. But I could not hate the Japanese. I had learned to love one Japanese family through my storybook friendship with Taro and Take. I could not suddenly learn to hate Japanese."[10]

In 1951 Earle, then on the faculty at Antioch College in Yellow Springs, Ohio, was offered a research position at the Atomic Bomb Casualty Commission (ABCC). The family took up residence on an American base near Kure and lived there for three years. Barbara volunteered at an orphanage and taught English to several young Japanese girls, but remembers having only a transient curiosity about the plight of hibakusha, a concern that was easily alleviated by the blithe assurances of Earle's colleagues that "things aren't as bad as you think" and "nobody is that sick."

It was in their dealings with ABCC that many hibakusha crystallized their feeling that they had been used as guinea pigs, "his-

torically rendered into expendable laboratory animals."[11] From its
physical location on Hijiyama Hill, built on the site of what had
been the Emperor Meiji's Hiroshima military headquarters (its construction required moving the remains in the military cemetery),
ABCC seemed to be a visual representation of American dominance over the ruined city. In Lifton's succinct phrase, it was a
"Kafkaesque" situation: "the nation which dropped the atomic
bombs sending its teams of physicians to make objective studies
of the weapon's initial and delayed medical effects."[12] The fact
that ABCC was under the auspices of the Atomic Energy Commission led to deeper suspicions, exacerbated by some elements of
the peace movement, about its possible hidden political or military
agendas.

Aside from these potent political symbols, hibakusha were
particularly angered by ABCC's policy of research without treatment, insensitive practices during examinations, and an aggressive
autopsy program that violated strongly held cultural taboos. Ironically Earle Reynolds was cited as particularly culpable in his
lack of sensitivity to subjects in his research study, which sought
to determine whether radiation exposure delayed the onset of
puberty:

> Largely at his instigation, the participants in the pediatric
> growth program were photographed in the nude in order
> to measure the possible effects of exposure on sexual mat-
> uration. Unlike statural or bodily growth and development,
> there are no simple quantitative measures of sexual matu-
> rity. Traditionally, it has been assessed by determining the age
> at which axillary and pubic hair appears, breast tissue starts
> to grow, menstruation begins, and the like. While he was at
> the Fels Institute, Earle had made an effort to develop a se-
> ries of developmental landmarks that could be scored from
> photographs. American children and their parents were gen-
> erally unconcerned about the use of this technique, but not
> so the Japanese, who objected to the photographs. Soon our
> contractors responsible for arranging appointments for the
> examinations brought word of increasing resistance to partic-
> ipation, particularly by teenaged girls. In time this aspect of
> his study was abandoned, but not before irreparable damage
> had been done. Even now, members of the Commission are
> occasionally pictured in the press as a group of aging voyeurs.
> Earle seemed oblivious to these problems.[13]

For many years Earle had dreamed of sailing around the world,
and the combination of low costs and superb craftsmanship in
post-Occupation Japan meant that he could afford to have a boat

built to the specifications of such a voyage. In October 1954 Barbara, Earle, Ted, Jessica, and a crew of three young Japanese men began that voyage on a fifty-foot yacht they had christened *Phoenix of Hiroshima*. Their port visits during that four-year voyage always generated significant attention, and from Tahiti to Hawaii they were besieged with questions about the atomic bomb. Thus it was that, far from Hiroshima, by listening to stories of the experiences of their crewmen and their families and friends, the Reynoldses came to understand something about the texture of hibakusha's daily life, of the social and economic discrimination they endured, and of their abiding desire for peace.

Initially surprised by the symbolism of reconciliation with which observers invested their journey, they came to accept and explore its possibilities. People "seemed to think it was very meaningful that Americans and Japanese had sailed together from Hiroshima in a ship named 'Phoenix.' They encouraged us in our plan to sail around the world together so many people would know about Hiroshima. We were not sailing to talk about Hiroshima. We thought we had left Hiroshima behind."[14]

Earle kept abreast of the scientific literature on radiation during port visits, but neither he nor Barbara was familiar with the work of American peace groups in opposing nuclear testing. In the spring of 1958 they were docked in Hawaii, preparing the *Phoenix* for its final return trip to Hiroshima, when they met Albert Bigelow, the captain of the *Golden Rule*.[15] The four crew members were Quaker activists who had announced their intention of sailing into the Pacific zone to protest the atmospheric testing of hydrogen weapons, but before their departure they were served with an injunction against sailing; despite this, they set sail and were arrested and charged with criminal contempt. They were sentenced to sixty days in jail.

Having absorbed and accepted the philosophic core of the protest, the Reynoldses and their one remaining Japanese companion, Niichi Mikami (whose mother and brother were hibakusha) felt called to complete that "forbidden voyage." Barbara was convinced of the moral rightness of the Quakers' cause, while Earle's decisions were shaped by his training as a scientist and a sailor. His concerns focused on the freedom of the seas, American responsibility for the welfare of the residents of the Trust territories, and, above all, his knowledge about the dangers of atmospheric radiation. His was no impulsive heroism, but a decided choice made against the certainty that any protest action would end his scientific and academic career. "I was born poor, worked hard, and have gone a long way farther than I could have expected; I hate to give it up."[16]

"I began to feel that God was speaking to us," Barbara wrote:

We had thought we were sailing around the world for our own pleasure but now it seemed that God had been preparing us for action. We had a sea-going yacht built in Hiroshima. We had sailed around the world as a family and had a companion who came from Hiroshima. During our voyage we had learned from our Japanese companions about the suffering which still continued in Hiroshima and Nagasaki.... We had learned what the people of other countries felt about the nuclear arms race.... My husband was a scientist with authority and experience.... We were already planning to return to Japan as we had promised to do.... "The forbidden zone" stretched directly across the natural route of a sailing vessel going to Japan from Hawaii.[17]

On June 27, 1958, the *Phoenix* was stopped at the edge of the "forbidden zone," and the next day, eighty-five miles inside the zone, two Coast Guard officers boarded the boat and arrested Earle, who was flown to Hawaii to stand trial. Barbara, Ted, and Niichi Mikami sailed the boat from Kwajalein (in the Marshall Islands) to Honolulu. They rented a small apartment on the outskirts of Waikiki and experienced an outpouring of material and moral support that sustained them during the two years it took for Earle's case to be resolved. It required two trials and two appeals before he was acquitted, using a defense that drew heavily on traditional arguments that guaranteed freedom of the seas. During those two years unacknowledged differences emerged from what had appeared a unified action:

My husband had become the spokesman for the *Phoenix* protest — and his reasons were not always the same as mine. He spoke of "freedom of the seas" and the extent to which science was being twisted for political ends, while I, as a woman, felt the need to emphasize the immorality of endangering life and the health of the world's children, including those yet to be born.

During the next two years, while my husband's conviction as a felon was under appeal, we were seemingly as close as ever. But the seeds of disunity had been sown.... Without being aware of my feelings, I resented the publicity that focused on my husband and did not recognize that... my function as secretary to send out fund appeals, prepare reports of progress, and write letters of thanks to contributors was equally as important as my husband's speaking tours and interviews with the media. Although I faithfully went through the motions, I was no longer a part of the team.[18]

The Reynoldses returned to Hiroshima in 1960 and were thrust into public prominence in the peace movement. Mary McMillan hired Earle to teach at Jogakuin and gave them emotional as well as economic assistance. It was her opinion that "the coming of Dr. Earle Reynolds and his family to Hiroshima in 1960 strengthened and gave more direction and unity to the city's peace movement than it had had for several years. Though the Reynoldses have not been completely understood even in Hiroshima, they have gradually gained the backing of most of the city's peace forces."[19] The Reynoldses sought some way to respond to the support and gratitude of hibakusha:

> A very lovely middle-aged woman came up to me and asked if I was Barbara Reynolds. When I said yes, she quietly drew back the sleeves of her beautiful kimono to expose a painful-looking thick keloid that completely covered her arm. Then, saying "Thank you very much," she bowed and slipped away into the crowd, leaving me standing, shocked, with tears overflowing my eyes.
>
> So many people seemed to feel that they had found a friend, someone who wanted to learn about their tragedy, someone who really cared and would try to communicate their hopes to other Americans who needed so much to be told. The responsibility was great. My heart was heavy with grief but I had no idea of how I could help. In the face of such suffering, such forgiveness, such trust, it was certainly not enough to say, "I'm sorry."[20]

The Reynoldses made the *Phoenix* their home. Earle not only taught at Jogakuin, but also developed a Peace Studies Institute at Hiroshima University and, with no little fortitude, wended his way through the minefield of competing interests that marked the organized peace movement in Japan. Barbara provided hospitality for the many visitors who made their way to the *Phoenix*, and sought to develop a style of peacemaking consistent both with her personality and deepening religiosity.

In October 1961, responding to the Soviet resumption of nuclear testing, the Reynoldses attempted to sail across the Japan Sea to Nakhodka to protest Soviet tests. Physically the voyage was hampered by harsh weather and dangerous seas (it was typhoon season) as well as complications secondary to having been denied visas to land in Nakhodka. This raised questions about whether they would be granted Japanese re-entry permits; these were, in fact, delayed. The announcement of their plan generated a passionate debate in Hiroshima, interesting for what it reveals about the

public perception of the Reynoldses. Friends opposed the plan out
of concern for their safety, but other observers were more cynical:

> A fairly large group of Hiroshima people argued that it was
> a terrible waste for the *Phoenix,* which they had come to
> consider as one of their own particular symbols for peace,
> to go forth into the Japan Sea, protesting against such heavy
> odds. It was like a drop in the bucket.... Some people were
> not even convinced of the purity of the Reynoldses' motives.
> Dr. Reynolds had said in *The Forbidden Voyage* that if any
> nation ever began to test nuclear weapons again, he would
> protest such an action as readily as he had protested Ameri-
> can tests. After all, they said, wasn't he really more interested
> in keeping his own vow than he was in the safety of his fam-
> ily or the effectiveness of the protest? Could it be that he was
> seeking his own glory?
>
> There were leftists who asked, "Aren't they going as Amer-
> ican spies?" And there were rightists who, some said, were
> eager to use the Reynoldses' voyage to support their own
> ideas vis-à-vis Russia. One person even asked, "since they're
> going to Russia, aren't they Communist sympathizers?"[21]

The Reynoldses had collected anti-nuclear letters and messages
from hibakusha and had promised to present these pleas to the
Russian people.

> When we finally arrived in sight of Nakhodka and were still
> several miles out, we were stopped by a Russian ship which
> ordered us to stop.
>
> An officer came on board. He spoke English very well and
> talked to us for a long time. He was polite and friendly but
> he refused to let us land. And he would not take the letters
> and messages we had brought.
>
> "The Russian people understand very well about Hiro-
> shima," he told us. "It is the Americans who must stop
> building nuclear weapons. The Russian people have had
> enough of war. We lost 20 million civilians in World War II.
> We only want to live in peace."[22]

The Peace Pilgrimage

While recovering from the physical and emotional difficulties of the
aborted journey (their rudder broke on the return to Japan, and
their yacht could have been destroyed on the rocks) Barbara was
haunted by a sense of responsibility for those undelivered pieces of

paper, mute symbols of hibakusha's need to speak to the world. Barbara and Jessica spent Christmas Day 1961 fasting in the Peace Park, praying to know how to respond to the trust hibakusha had exhibited in entrusting those messages to them.

> By the end of the day, I knew that God wanted us to send the same messages, the messages of the hibakusha, to both the USSR and the U.S. in such a way that all the people of the world could hear. This meant that the letters must go to the American and Soviet Embassies at the United Nations and they must be taken there by hibakusha who would represent Hiroshima and Nagasaki and could speak on behalf of all the atomic bomb survivors.[23]

The fruit of that prayer was a five-month, twelve-nation Peace Pilgrimage undertaken the next year by Barbara, Miyoko Matsubara, and Hiromasa Hanabusa (Hiro).[24] Barbara's opposition to nuclear weapons gained its passion from her personal encounter with hibakusha, and the genius of the Peace Pilgrimage was its simple and decent replication of that experience for others. Inherent to the nature of the pilgrimage was forging a new relationship between hibakusha and Americans, a recasting of roles that had previously been rigidly defined by the constraints of conventional charity.

If the voyage of the *Phoenix* had introduced Barbara to the complexity of Hiroshima's story, this pilgrimage allowed her both to deepen her empathy and to understand the impact hibakusha had on their listeners. She accompanied Hiro and Miyoko as a companion and aide, helping to negotiate travel plans, arranging speaking engagements, and acting as a cultural translator.[25] At the same time she was groping for a definition of the role she might play. She was not amassing information about Hiroshima so that she could, in turn, speak about the bomb. The few talks she gave inevitably engendered accusations about her lack of patriotism, but audience response to Miyoko was different: "hearts were opened listening to her." Barbara conceived of the pilgrimage as a "people to people mission," the crafting of an essential partnership ("they have the knowledge, we have the weapons") in the fight against nuclear weapons.

Miyoko, a hibakusha, had been twelve at the time of the bombing, one of the many children her age working to tear down buildings to create fire lanes in the center of the city. Hiro, who had been evacuated from Hiroshima with his elderly grandmother, was orphaned at the age of two when his parents died in the aftermath of the atomic bomb. Hiro and his grandmother faced innumerable obstacles in the harsh poverty of the post-war years, but "they were a team," and despite a deprivation of material goods Hiro experienced an upbringing marked by abundant affection. ("The only people who are poor," his grandmother told him, "are those who want more than they have.")[26]

In contrast, Miyoko knew only terrible, unending abandonment. Like all hibakusha, she suffered from societal discrimination, but her severe losses at such a critical age were exacerbated by the unkindness of her family ("better if you died, you're so scarred," Barbara reported that Miyoko's mother said to her). An elder brother and his wife died from radiation sickness, her father died of cancer (presumed to have been related to the bomb), and Miyoko felt a strong sense of responsibility to care for her mother and three surviving younger siblings. At the time of the Peace Pilgrimage she was working at an orphanage (established by Rev. Tanimoto) for children blinded by the bomb. Miyoko was fiercely self-conscious about her severe keloid scarring: she had applied to the Hiroshima Maidens Project but was rejected, and her work with these blind children provided a respite from the vicious stares of strangers.

The opportunity to be a peace pilgrim gave Miyoko a special task, a sense of mission, and an intimacy with Barbara that offered a tentative amelioration of her profound loneliness. It is sadly ironic that Miyoko had to travel to other countries to receive love and concern, paradoxical that the very experience that led to her isolation was that which rewarded her with attention and affection. The confluence of these hidden emotions would be masked by the ambivalence that marked the relationship between Barbara and Miyoko, a love-hate, mother-daughter bond that was powerfully magnetic and resonant with grief.

Their relationship was complicated even further by the jealousy that greeted Miyoko when she returned to Hiroshima. Physically exhausted by the demands of travel, emotionally drained by the constant reiteration of her story and that of other hibakusha, Miyoko wanted only to escape to the anonymity of the orphanage. Other hibakusha, envious of the attention she had received, demanded her continued involvement with the peace movement. Many also presumed, wrongfully, that she had received gifts and money (abiding by rigorous rules they refused even token gifts). She was accused of being a "professional hibakusha" (those who have gained prominence because of the frequency with which they speak, and who thus provide the lens through which outsiders perceive Hiroshima), of "selling the bomb" for financial and emotional gain. Ironically, Miyoko would later direct those same accusations against Barbara, particularly after she became an honorary citizen.

Miyoko would continue to be shunned by other hibakusha; despite involvement with a number of private and official hibakusha associations (she was, for some time, employed at the Hiroshima Peace Memorial Museum), Miyoko has remained painfully lonely and isolated from her natural community, an isolation that is worsened by her emotional lability and excessive need for attention. In this Miyoko mirrored Barbara's situation, for although Barbara was endowed with much greater emotional and spiritual resources, she would know a similar isolation from her peers in the historic peace churches. Although she would occasionally act in concert with others, Barbara remained a lone figure. She was hurt by the mockery of people who accused her of being a "professional Hiroshima person," yet in her peripatetic activism her life mirrored the isolation of hibakusha. The integrity of Barbara's passionate commitment was, on occasion, diluted by actions that revealed a striking naivete of judgment, a willingness to trust people who proved less than trustworthy. A woman of Barbara's age had her expectations shaped by societal attitudes that accorded diminished seriousness to a woman's work, and these cyclical excursions into a disingenuous innocence may have reflected a temporary retreat from the rigorous demands of the tasks she set for herself.

Denied affection from her peers, Miyoko expected that Barbara would continue to provide the responsive attention she had received on that first Peace Pilgrimage. Barbara did feel a sense of responsibility to Miyoko, and part of her self-sacrifice was to listen to Miyoko rage against her bomb experience and the years of grief it ushered in. Traveling in Holland in 1962, Barbara was overwhelmed by Miyoko's constant reiteration of how "everything is spoiled" in her life because of the keloid scars that resulted from her burns. They were talking in the kitchen of the home where they were staying, waiting for water to boil on an old stove, when Barbara felt "an almost irresistible desire to jam my hand down on that hot stove and say, 'You know, scarring doesn't have to destroy your life. If I could change things for you by scarring myself I'd do it.' "[27]

No less than Miyoko, Barbara would later romanticize and yearn for the purity of intent and response of that first modest journey when through their personality differences Barbara came to understand that the atomic bomb incurred a far more grievous maiming than conventional weapons ("Miyoko could never get enough attention," she said, "but Hiro could never give enough"). "I was beginning to realize how important it was for hibakusha to talk directly to people of other countries so they could realize how different atomic bombs are from any other weapon." When people in Europe spoke of the bombing they had endured, Hiro reminded them "that they did not have to be afraid of A-bomb disease or of radiation effects which might cause damage to their children and grandchildren."[28]

Barbara's reflections on the Peace Pilgrimage affirm Lifton's observation that in their dealings with hibakusha Americans expect either seething hostility or none at all. She describes one talk at a large metropolitan high school:

> The entire audience...sat motionless as she talked. I could see Miyoko's anguish reflected in their eyes. She described her classmates jumping from a high bridge into the river, their clothes and flesh burned from their bodies. Her voice rose to a childlike pitch of relieved hysteria as she told how her friends were calling in vain for their mothers: "Okaasan! Okaasan! Tasukete kure!" Come and help me! Then she broke down, excused herself, and came back to huddle in her seat. There was a period of stunned silence. No one moved, not even to wipe away the tears. At last,...a student asked, "Do you hate the Americans very much?"
>
> The question broke the silence, but the group reaction was so strange as to be almost unbelievable. A ripple of spontaneous *laughter* swept across the auditorium, a nervous, compulsive giggle.

It was Hiro who answered, his voice "clipped and authoritative":

> "Before we came on this trip...we talked to hundreds of survivors...we asked all of them the same question, 'How do you feel about the United States? Do you hate Americans?' And always they said, 'No, we don't hate the Americans any more — but we *do hate nuclear weapons!* And WE HATE WAR...."
>
> Tension, rejection and potential violence were dissolved as the entire student body rose to its feet....They had braced themselves for hatred and had been met with love. That survivors of Hiroshima, with so much reason for bitterness and hate, had brought a message of concern for humanity had touched the wellsprings of idealism and good.[29]

The World Friendship Center

Barbara repeatedly said that "people find in Hiroshima what they are looking for," and she was no exception. Both from religious conviction and an inherent idealism Barbara had a profound need to find hope in Hiroshima. She reiterated that message of hope as if a mantra, only on occasion admitting to fatigue over the "despair that people clutched to themselves"[30] when hearing hibakusha speak.

Barbara hoped to multiply the positive impact of the Peace Pilgrimage with the far more ambitious World Peace Study Mission of 1964. She specifically wanted to invite mature professionals who could speak to their peers in other countries and return to Japan with an experience of international cooperation.

> I think of the many like Miyoko who have been able to survive only by sealing off memory, as nature builds scar tissue over a gaping wound, but who tore open those wounds so that their representatives of the Peace Pilgrimage would be amply prepared to testify to the continuing inhumanity of nuclear war. Their purpose? Not to accuse. Not to ask pity. Not even, primarily, to appeal for help. (What help is there for them, who are already doomed?) But in the hope that understanding of their suffering may save others from a similar fate, to insure that no one else, anywhere, will ever know the tragedy of nuclear war — or prepare to inflict it on others.

Her goal was "peace *through* friendship" (emphasis hers).

> How wonderful for them — and for their hosts — *if two or three [hibakusha] who have felt themselves alone and forgotten* could be invited to spend a week or two as honored guests in a foreign community where, with the help of an interpreter-companion, they could exchange ideas, *receive the love and concern of many,* and . . . convey the facts about the condition of A-bomb survivors to people everywhere. . . . Perhaps, in this way, it may yet be possible to reach those thousands who are still unable to grasp the meaning of the nuclear age and who speak glibly in terms of "casualties" and "percentages of survival." (emphasis added)[31]

Twenty-five hibakusha, among whom were ministers, physicians, writers, educators, and social workers, accompanied by translators and tour organizers, traveled to eighteen countries, including all of the nuclear nations, on a rigorous three-month journey fraught with logistical and organizational difficulties.

> I was stubborn. I was so sure that my own ideas were right that I refused to listen to the advice of friends. . . . Instead of waiting [until after the 1964 U.S. presidential elections] . . . I used most of the rest of my inheritance to purchase air tickets for the entire group [estimated by one Japanese as costing $50,000–$60,000[32]]. Now people would know we were

really coming! Now they would have to get ready for us because we were on our way to bring universal peace to the world.[33]

When she wrote about the Peace Study Mission she attributed its failure to her lack of spiritual maturity.

Because the first Peace Pilgrimage had been successful, I began to plan a new and larger one, but this time I did not spend quiet days of prayer in preparation. I was like someone who has received the command to build a house and, eagerly, without waiting for a detailed design or consulting the wishes of the master, rushes to construct something according to his own ideas! What a miserable and unstable house it was and yet, how magnificent it might have been if all of us who took part had joined together for even one day of meditation and prayer in the Peace Park before we left.[34]

Barbara returned to Hiroshima emotionally exhausted and facing the impending public announcement that her twenty-nine-year marriage was ending in divorce. "I was ashamed that throughout our travels for peace I had not been honest about the fact that my family was not truly united as everyone believed. I did not know where to go or what to do. Even the *Phoenix* was no longer my home. My world had gone to pieces around me."[35] Stripped of security, comfort, and purpose, her descent into radical physical and emotional poverty loosened parched soil and prepared her to receive a Word of equally radical faith and hope. Barbara came to believe that these profound losses resulted from her willful disobedience "to a God who was both merciful and just, the God whom Jesus made known. Obedience until death — one's own or the death of one's loved ones.... It was doubt which had cut me off to walk in darkness, even while I claimed to be walking in the light.... Now through that darkness, shone a single ray of hope."[36]

With streams of living water, God answered me. No polluted canals or brackish pools. No chlorinated, metered flow nor trickle from a rusty pipe, but a torrent, ever renewing itself, bringing life to my parched soul. How I longed to share it with others who, like myself, had rejected Christ, having failed to see Him in some who called themselves Christian. How many, I wondered, had turned away from Him because of my divided life?

But God forgave me everything! Light, like a sunrise, dispelled the darkness.[37]

As her grief abated, Barbara came to see her loss as an opportunity to develop empathy for hibakusha, who had known an infinitely greater, more total loss. In time hibakusha identified with her vulnerability, respected her commitment to peace, and admired her embrace of voluntary poverty as an expression of her religious beliefs. "The Japanese have never been blind to how Barbara-san, a foreigner, has sacrificed her home, property and reputation for the sake of the A- and H-bombs prohibition campaign and peace movement, as well as for the relief of survivors."[38]

A time of retreat and physical recuperation followed her conversion ("I asked God to make me well"), and then Barbara returned to Hiroshima where, aided by American friends, she established the World Friendship Center. From its beginning, the Center had a decidedly non-institutional focus. "There was a very long statement of objectives and goals, but no constitution or rules for the organization itself. Anyone who attended a meeting became a member, sometimes even an officer. For the first five years there were no membership dues and the Center existed on free-will contributions, mostly from Barbara's friends."[39]

It was perhaps this very loose structure that allowed the Center to develop into the binational effort it is today. An American committee was established in 1968, and to this day it provides fundraising and publicity, organizes speaking tours for visiting hibakusha, and chooses the American resident directors, most of whom have been retired professionals, members of historic peace churches. They are assisted by bi-lingual Japanese volunteers. Ongoing decisions are made by members of the Rijikai, the Japanese board of directors.

The activities of the Friendship Center in Hiroshima have changed over the years, but its essence has remained constant: involvement in peace activities, support for hibakusha, including regular visits to nursing homes and hospitals, and translation of material related to the bomb. Staff members offer moderately priced English lessons to Japanese of all ages and oversee numerous cultural activities, with particular importance given to the binational Teacher Exchange Program (TEP). It also offers moderately priced hostel accommodations for international and Japanese visitors to Hiroshima.

Ironically, one of the first decisions of the American Committee was to recommend that Barbara return to the United States so that the Center could develop an autonomous institutional identity. That move was personally difficult for Barbara but proved to be a healthy one for the Center. Prior to her departure a newspaper article by a Japanese reporter, whom Barbara characterized as melodramatic and sentimental, distressed Barbara's friends and admirers with its suggestion that she was leaving because of "disappointment" with the Japanese peace movement. She was im-

mensely grateful for the generous gifts she received at a farewell
testimonial dinner, at which Mayor Setsuo Yamada presented her
with a silver key to Hiroshima.

Barbara left Hiroshima in March 1969 and spent a year at Pen-
dle Hill, a Quaker study center in Wallingford, Pennsylvania, not
far from Philadelphia, where she studied writing with Elizabeth
Gray Vining.[40] She had intended to write a book about peace and
intercultural understanding, but that never materialized. Instead,
she began what would be a four-year effort to find a home for the
boxes of bomb-related material she had brought back to the United
States. In 1973 she was introduced to Professors Canby Jones
and Larry Gara at Wilmington College, a small Quaker college
in Wilmington, Ohio, and their enthusiastic personal and institutional support led to the establishment of the Hiroshima/Nagasaki
Memorial Collection.

The collection has three foci: memorabilia and literature about
the hibakusha experience, materials documenting the dangers of
atomic energy and nuclear weapons, and materials about the
peace movement, including some of the Reynoldses' personal papers, notably those that related to the voyage of the *Phoenix*.
Its purpose is to "memorialize — to keep alive the memory — of
Hiroshima/Nagasaki and what happened there. The intention was
to let the voices of the hibakusha be heard and to encourage research into that aspect and its influence on the growth of peace
consciousness."[41]

Barbara moved from Ann Arbor, Michigan, where she had been
living with her son, Ted, and his family, to Wilmington. The college
provided her with a dorm room, meals in the college cafeteria, and
a monthly stipend while she catalogued the collection and organized an impressive "Thirty Years After Conference" (1975), which
was attended by prominent Japanese peace and hibakusha activists.
Barbara remained at Wilmington until 1978, when a full-time faculty director was hired; the following year the college inaugurated
a peace studies program and began the development of the Peace
Resource Center. Since then the Center has been under the able
direction of Helen Redding Wiegel.

Ambiguous Symbols

Barbara's peace work was motivated by her religious beliefs, and
she specifically sought a Quaker institution as the home for the
Hiroshima/Nagasaki Memorial Collection. Explicit references to
her faith were somewhat problematic for some Hiroshima observers. One Japanese activist recently referred to the Friendship

Center as "an American colony," staffed by people from a "Christian, missionary background," peripheral to Hiroshima's concerns, conveying the wrong impression of Hiroshima so that visitors left with their consciences "cleansed."[42] While I do not know how widespread his attitude is, it does raise important questions about Barbara's persistence in viewing Hiroshima through Christian lenses. So central was this commitment that she could say that "one of the terrible results of the bomb was that it impeded missionary efforts because a Christian nation had dropped the bomb."

The majority of Hiroshima residents are adherents of the Shinran sect of Buddhism. The prophet Shinran (1173–1262), the sect's founder, was about to enter heaven when, moved by the suffering of those who remained on earth, he returned to guide them. Shinran is an engaged Buddhism, with an element of witness that easily appealed to hibakusha. Nevertheless, Barbara's more elegiac writings framed Hiroshima's narrative within a specific Christian formulation.

> Hiroshima has become like a second home to me. The hibakusha seem like a part of my family. I know they are very precious to God and I want them to be a part of His family too. Through their experience and their dedication to tell everyone in the world what happened so that no one else will ever suffer as they have suffered, they are an important part of God's plan. They show us the terrible evil of which mankind is capable. I pray that they will also come to know God, through His Son, Jesus Christ. Only then will they be able to present the whole message: the warning and the hope.[43]

Barbara's belief in the redemptive nature of hibakusha suffering suffused her understanding of Hiroshima's role:

> Somehow, through their descent into the crucible of agony, the hibakusha *as a group* have emerged with a compassion that cannot be explained by human reason or logic. They have been touched by a concern beyond the imagining of mortal man, by a Spirit that loves us and requires us to love one another, that forgives us, and expects us to forgive each other....
>
> Through the hibakusha, themselves still tormented and without hope, is revealed the existence of a Power in the universe that *does indeed* care for man! I have seen human beings everywhere respond to this message with newly-awakened hope and dedication, *although the hibakusha*

*themselves were not aware of the Power behind their ap-
peal* [emphasis added]. Through them, the Spirit speaks —
and there is Something in the hearts of men everywhere that
responds.[44]

Lifton found "a public image of hibakusha as people who, having suffered grievously, were now totally dedicated to an altruistic
mission of saving the rest of the world from similar suffering — an
image which, at least in its pure form, we have seen to be simply
not in accord with the complexities of human behavior."[45] This is
the image that Barbara sought to inculcate by her eloquent writing
and the witness of the Peace Pilgrimages. A certain amount of such
missionary spirit is, of course, inevitable, given the self-selection
process by which those hibakusha who choose to travel abroad are
precisely the people motivated by that sense of mission. Despite,
or perhaps because of, an inevitable ambivalence in such a complex relationship, there were times when she tended to romanticize
hibakusha, to perceive them as pure and selfless, as if their virtue
ameliorated our responsibility for the act that initiated their suffering. She did understand that suffering can lead, not to nobility of
heart, but to a profound self-absorption. She writes of the response
of hibakusha to the visit of the Vietnamese Buddhist monk, Thich
Nhat Hanh:

> I saw tears of compassion in the eyes of hibakusha...who
> for too long have been sealed in the prison of their own
> self-commiseration. I knew then that what Nhat Hanh had
> brought was what they needed: an awareness of the sufferings
> of others that would rip apart the shell of despair, hopeless-
> ness and defeat — an identification with humanity that would
> draw them out of their own emotional isolation.[46]

Barbara's insistence on the Christian meaning of Hiroshima
ironically obscured the potential and actual reconciliation that accrued from her involvement with hibakusha. A Japanese physician
friend once told Barbara that Hiroshima had obligations (*on*) to
her. The Japanese recognize two types of debts: *gimu,* which is
owed to ancestors and parents, and so can never be exhausted,
and *giri,* obligations incurred from benefactors in the commerce of
ordinary daily life, which must be promptly and exactly repaid.[47]

Through her embrace of voluntary poverty and her emotional
vulnerability, Barbara became the American to whom hibakusha
could repay the *on* that had been accrued from having received
charity at their time of great need and thus begin to negotiate a
more equitable relationship with Americans. In addition to their
emotional identification with her, hibakusha felt a very practical

sense of indebtedness to Barbara because she had spent almost her entire inheritance to fund the World Peace Study Mission. The Japanese could not understand why Barbara had spent the money on them and had not saved it for her children, and therefore they felt profoundly obligated to her. Barbara experienced considerable conflict about the many gifts she received and she angered supporters who gave her money, expecting it would be used for her needs, only to find that she would pass it on to others she deemed more worthy of assistance.[48]

Barbara had a sophisticated theoretical understanding of *on* and cast the relationship between hibakusha and victims of the bomb into that paradigm: hibakusha's sense of personal mission evolved from their deeply felt obligations to carry the message of the suffering of those who did not survive.

> The most terrible thing about nuclear weapons is that the atomic bomb not only will destroy humanity, but that it will destroy all *humanity.*
>
> At the time that the A-bomb was dropped, it was so incomprehensible, so vastly more destructive than anything human beings had ever known. The instant obliteration of all that human beings had ever known, the immediate being surrounded by the death and the dying and the hopeless situation where no one was able to act as a human being; nobody was able to help others; people had to leave their loved ones trapped in houses pinned under immovable debris. They could not respond as human beings and were in such a state of total shock that they responded to the instinct for personal survival....And for years after that they lived with the psychological and emotional problems, the guilt, the memory of what they had to leave behind them — with the sense that they should have done something.
>
> They say, "I passed this person crying out for water. I passed this person crying out to be helped to a hospital. I passed by and I didn't help." But gradually they realized that they could not be blamed. It was the Atomic Bomb which had done this to them. What they have suffered from, far more than the radiation fears, which are very real, is that they failed to be human beings. And in order to regain their humanity they have to fight with everything that is in them, against nuclear weapons. Nuclear weapons are the enemy. That is what is going to destroy, or has already destroyed our humanity.[49]

In a 1979 letter to the writer William Bradford Hue, Barbara commented that she had been "set up as an idol" and knew "the profound damage of what this can do to a human being, and how difficult it is to escape from those who need to create a symbol." Barbara chafed at the confining restrictions of her symbolic role even as she understood how important it was to respect hibakusha perceptions.

> When Joan Baez came over [in 1968] the first thing they did, when they met her at the airport, they wanted to take her right to the Peace Park to pray for the dead. She said no, she didn't want to do that. And I think she tried to explain that she just didn't want to, that she felt it would be kind of false and a publicity-seeking sort of thing to go out there and have pictures taken of her, bowing in front of the Cenotaph and praying, and she told us when she came to the Center that she just wanted to walk there quietly by herself in the evening or in the morning and experience her own feelings, her own privacy. But to the Japanese that meant that she didn't care and that it was a rebuff really. And they said, "Why did she come here if she is so much for peace, and she didn't even pay her respects at the Peace Park?" So there again it was just a matter of cultural misunderstanding. But the hibakusha in the hospitals who were watching the TV, watching her arrival and then expecting to see her go to the Peace Park, . . . were very upset that she didn't. So it's just one of those things. . . . We don't think that praying in public or laying a wreath on the tomb of the Unknown Soldier is a necessary thing to say that we really feel deeply about what's happened. But again, it's a symbol. And the symbol to Hiroshima was important.[50]

Barbara's actions alternately revealed exquisite cultural sensitivity or an equally astounding obtuseness. It was the latter attitude that fueled her persistence in developing self-help programs for hibakusha, work projects that would allow them the opportunity to perform simple, safe labor for a modest salary.

Hibakusha were eligible for welfare assistance, but accepting it meant being subject to the scrutiny of both government social workers and sharply critical neighbors. To avoid this stigma, many hibakusha accepted work as day laborers in government programs (similar to WPA and CCC projects during the Depression), physically demanding jobs that exacerbated bomb-related health problems, leaving some of them, particularly women, unable to work more than two or three days a week. Japanese peace activists and some hibakusha organizations argued that hibakusha's penurious existence was a visible condemnation of the government's failure to meet its responsibilities to them, a mute protest of symbolic reproach. Barbara was deeply distressed by the plight of these infirm hibakusha and struggled to develop home-based industries that, though based on traditional Japanese crafts, were modeled on Western charities.

In 1965 she proposed putting together packets of origami cranes: an explanation of the legend of the thousand cranes, the story of Sadako Sasaki,[51] and, instead of an instruction sheet with directions for folding cranes, actual samples of what each step in the folding process would look like. These would be sold for a modest amount (twenty-five cents) with twenty cents profit going to the hibakusha. The peace group SANE (Citizens for a SANE Nuclear Policy) contacted the Friendship Center and requested ten thousand of these packets for a large rally, but before the order could be met, word of the project provoked a confrontation with Ichiro Kawamoto.[52]

Kawamoto is the founder and inspiration of the Folded Crane Club, begun in 1958 and dedicated to the memory of Sadako. Kawamoto was the person most responsible for the construction of the Children's Monument in the Peace Park, and he has worked tirelessly on behalf of ill and infirm hibakusha. His passionate political opposition to nuclear weapons has not detracted from a sincere care and attention to individuals. With the young junior high school girls who are the club's members, Kawamoto visits hibakusha in their homes and hospitals, and they fold paper cranes with which to welcome visitors to Hiroshima and to be sent around the world as a prayer for peace. Barbara respected Kawamoto as one of her teachers and so was distressed by the stern fury and deep offense with which he responded to her project. Although she hoped that a change from origami cranes to balls would ameliorate his criticism, he angrily refused her apologies. "There can't be any reconciliation because you can't make up for the fact that you were willing to sell paper cranes," he said, at the conclusion of a meeting set up to resolve the conflict. Barbara's translator turned to her and said, "The real problem is that you are an American; there is nothing you can do about this." "I just sat there and cried," Barbara said, and in 1989, relating the incident to me, she wept again at her remembered grief and frustration.[53]

This encounter can be seen as a paradigm of the encounters between hibakusha and an American as visible as Barbara Reynolds. Just as Barbara's relationship with Miyoko is emblematic of that between Americans and Japanese, her effort to serve hibakusha illuminates the minefield of expectations in that complex, fluid relationship.

There are peace groups who have used hibakusha as symbols of the terrible consequences of nuclear war; in a curious way, telling their unique and passionate stories reconfines them to a painful anonymity. Just as once, as residents of an enemy population, hibakusha were objects to military and political planners, they can again lose individuality when they are seen as lessons of war's most savage progression. Barbara Reynolds also became a symbol, and she too was forced to surrender her individuality. Just as hibakusha have allowed others to appropriate the facts of their city to myths, so Barbara presented herself to be a foil for anger and a presence for healing.

Barbara Reynolds sought to be a symbol of "the power of Jesus Christ," but the people of Hiroshima saw and experienced her as a symbolic American. There are wounds of history that cannot be assuaged by acts of charity or words of sorrow offered by citizens of the nation that inflicted those wounds. Barbara knew the inherent impotence of these actions, but she also knew that some response was necessary. She understood the limits of empathy, how impossible it was to know either the depth of hibakusha's grief or the loneliness of the isolation imposed by illness and discrimination. She understood the limits of action, and she chafed against her inability to assuage the poverty and hardship of individual hibakusha, an impatience that could lead to misguided programs, particularly when she made decisions without a careful consideration of Japanese culture.

Barbara Reynolds's actions were specific to Hiroshima, but in many ways she was an estimable model for a social activist. She listened to hibakusha with patience, respect, and compassion. She was faithful to her commitment for decades and willingly endured the countless small sacrifices that expressed her care, whether it required that she sit at an airport for three hours or testify at the United Nations. Barbara's political radicalism was tempered by her religious convictions and her acceptance of a traditional, nurturing feminine role; what emerged was a theology of reconciliation that was lived through presence, friendship, and availability.

4

The Betrayal of Loyalty

AMERICAN HIBAKUSHA

———— ☞ ————

My name is Jane Yoshiko Iwashika. I was born in Fresno, California, in 1927. In 1938, before the war between Japan and the United States had started, I went to Japan with my grandfather and sister. My sister was ill; she had a sinus problem and something like an ulcer, and my grandfather decided to take her to Japan for a cure. She needed company, so I tagged along. I thought it would be fun to go someplace different, but I didn't know Japan was so far away. I thought it was close, like San Francisco. My sister's health began to improve, but by then the war had started and we had to stay there. We were stranded.

In San Francisco, in 1988, I attended the annual commemoration service that American hibakusha hold on August 6. The Japanese and Japanese American communities of San Francisco also have an annual event in August, a cultural festival held in Japantown. The Committee of Atomic Bomb Survivors in the United States (CABS), which organized the commemoration, had requested that the larger festival be postponed to the following weekend to honor the solemnity of their service, but the request was denied. A small group of American hibakusha gathered in an unadorned meeting room on the second floor of a bank building to conduct an austerely sober memorial service with readings, speeches, and prayers that were punctuated by the discordant sounds of music and laughter drifting up from the streets below. I took the noise to be an unwelcome distraction but later came to understand it as a fitting aural representation of the isolation of American hibakusha.

The Japanese-American community had much to celebrate in 1988; after a twelve-year effort they had obtained redress for the internment camps of World War II. The process of achieving redress, which included political lobbying and public hearings, allowed Japanese Americans to voice their personal and communal anger and sorrow. Living survivors received a token compensation ($20,000) for lost property and income and an official apology from the government.

The public resolution of what President Reagan called a "sad chapter in American history" must have also lifted some of the private burdens of those Japanese Americans who endured the dislocation of the internment camps.

> The truth was that the government we trusted had betrayed us. Acknowledging such a reality was so difficult that our natural feelings of rage, fear, and helplessness were turned inward and buried. When human beings experience betrayal by a trusted source, it leads to deep depression, a sense of shame, a sense of "there must be something wrong with me." We were ashamed and humiliated; it was too painful to see that the government was not helping us, but was in fact against us. We used psychological defense mechanisms such as repression, denial, rationalization, and identification with the aggressor to defend ourselves against the devastating reality of what was being done to us.[1]

Redress was an acknowledgment of the government's wrongdoing, and as a result "denial and rationalization are no longer necessary defenses. Japanese Americans can feel an inner sense of honor and integrity that is validated and confirmed by the larger society."[2]

Many Japanese-American families were separated by circumstances during the war, and the experience of those in the United States — relocation, internment, military service — was radically different from that of their relatives who were stranded in Japan. Redress may have restored a sense of community and autonomy for those who experienced internment, but for those who survived the atomic bombings of Hiroshima and Nagasaki the war will never be over.

If the tumultuous history between Japan and the United States is a tornado, then American hibakusha are those who have been caught up by the funnel cloud. They, like other hibakusha, wonder when and how their radiation exposure will affect their health, but unlike hibakusha who live in Japan, they must also worry about the cost of medical care and the lack of physicians specializing in radiation-related diseases. They, like other Japanese Americans, have had to contend with the effects of this country's pernicious anti-Asian racism, but the very existence of American hibakusha reopens the passions of the war and the impossible demands of proving loyalty that were imposed on their community.

American hibakusha were born in this country but are deeply imbued with the cultural ethos of Japan, and this Japanese ethos has informed the way in which they have sought to achieve a measure of justice for themselves.[3] American hibakusha have had few political successes, and the narrative of their organizing effort reveals an almost embarrassing weakness and a failure to accomplish their goals. They are clearly uncomfortable with an aggressive insistence on their rights, which has been the traditional way that victims have sought to rectify situations of injustice in the United States.

Rather than relying on the confrontational manner in which Americans seek "rights" and claim justice, Japanese society places a strong emphasis on *amae,* an appeal based on interdependence. Takeo Doi, M.D., a Japanese psychiatrist, considers *amae* unique to the Japanese psychology, and he relates it to the uniqueness of Japanese language. "The typical psychology of a given nation can be learned only through familiarity with its native language. The language comprises everything which is intrinsic to the soul of a nation and therefore provides the best projective test there is for each nation."[4] John Bester, the translator of Doi's seminal work, offers a succinct summary of this concept.

> The Japanese term *amae* refers, initially, to the feelings that all normal infants at the breast harbor toward the mother — dependence, the desire to be passively loved, the unwillingness to be separated from the warm mother-child circle and cast into a world of objective "reality."
>
> On the personal level, this means that within his own most intimate circle, and to diminishing degrees outside that circle, he seeks relationships that, however binding they may be in their outward aspects, allow him to presume, as it were on familiarity. . . .
>
> . . . It is obvious, for example, that where *amae* is so important to the individual the organization of society as a whole will take corresponding account of the individual's needs. To the insider, this thoughtfulness of society will seem particularly warm and "human"; to the outsider, it may seem to encourage self-indulgence and subjectivity.[5]

Dr. Doi's concept is key in understanding the strategy that American hibakusha have chosen, an appeal to goodness and a sense of community. The public testimony of American hibakusha reveals their desire to be treated with sincerity and compassion. The appeal to helplessness is entirely consistent with *amae,* but it is jarring to an American audience that is accustomed to achieve social progress by making claims based on justice. CABS leader Kanji Kuramoto exemplified this attitude when he addressed a California legislative committee hearing in May 1974 and began his testimony: "I do not want to *beg* for your support, but I am appealing to open your hearts to aid these people in the spirit of true love."[6]

Different cultural teachings are only one of the daunting organizational obstacles faced by American hibakusha, which include their small numbers, geographic isolation, and lack of fluency in English, but probably the most formidable barrier to communicating their story has been the persistent myths about who they are and how they came to be bombed by their own government. A 1972 *Newsweek* article, which began with this stunningly inaccurate paragraph, is symptomatic of the misinformation that has dogged American hibakusha:

> They call themselves the American hibakusha — literally, the "receive bomb people" — and for more than 26 years, they have lived lives of quiet desperation. While a chastened U.S. government lavished free medical care on survivors of Hiroshima and Nagasaki, the American hibakusha — Japanese too, but living in the U.S. — remained unnoticed and uncared for.[7]

The United States government has never acted "chastened" over the use of the atomic bomb, and while millions of dollars have been spent (hardly lavished) in support of the Atomic Bomb Casualty Commission, the Commission's facilities are strictly for research, not treatment. Hibakusha do receive free care at the Atomic Bomb Hospitals; these were built by Japanese citizens with proceeds from the New Year postal lottery and are operated under the auspices of the Japan Red Cross Society.

There is a widespread perception that the very presence of American hibakusha in Japan during the war was proof of disloyalty. Dorothy Stroup, a Berkeley author who wrote an article about American hibakusha in 1978, received hate mail that asked, "If these people were really Americans, what were they *doing* over there?"[8]

It has been difficult for American hibakusha to undertake the political activism that has sustained many of their Japanese and Korean peers. The very existence of American hibakusha seems to provoke a heightened emotional response from listeners. Rinjiro Sodei, a Japanese historian and writer, speculated about this dynamic:

> In the country which caused the atomic disaster, for anyone to step forward and announce that he was one of the surviving victims was an act that required the utmost courage. The existence of living evidence of the A-bomb disaster in

the form of a human being who had experienced it would arouse in the perpetrators a sense of guilt which they have always sought to push down into some remote corner of their subconscious. The hibakusha are living reminders of the barbarous act which was committed against humanity.[9]

The strategies that CABS has adopted have been partially determined by the ethos of the wider Japanese-American community, whose official organizations have been slow to support American hibakusha. It is understandable that they are eager to avoid a discussion of the bomb, given the treatment that Nisei (second-generation Japanese Americans) experienced during the war. (Their parents, the Issei generation, were the Japanese immigrants to the United States.) The Sansei (third generation) are much more outspoken than their parents' generation, more willing to identify and confront attitudes that are the legacy of anti-Japanese racism. These strong generational differences are based in the error of "presentism" and "pastism," and it is the latter belief that has skewed the actions of American hibakusha.

Michael Banton defines presentism as the tendency "to interpret other historical periods in terms of the concepts, values and understanding of the present." Therefore, Japanese Americans growing up in an era of free speech, dissent, confrontation, and legal redress find it difficult to understand behavior from another era where the interaction was based primarily on domination.

Pastism refers to the tendency to interpret the present in terms of the concepts, values, and governance of the past. As opposed to presentism, it sees yesterday's model as the present-day reality. Therefore, individuals who grew up under domination . . . behave in a fashion more appropriate to a past era. For example, some Nisei find it difficult to talk about the wartime evacuation and to support a call for financial redress, partly because of the fear that taking a stand on "unpopular issues" would be treated in the same manner that they had experienced in the 1930s.[10]

Until 1977, when a team of Japanese physicians began the first of what has become biennial visits, American hibakusha had no regular access to physical and laboratory examination by medical personnel knowledgeable about the effects of radiation exposure. Their anxieties about atomic bomb–related diseases are compounded by the fact that commercial insurance companies do not provide coverage for diseases caused by an act of war. Consequently, they face potentially catastrophic health costs if they develop a disease that is linked to their radiation exposure. Legislation on their behalf has been filed almost annually since 1972, but all the bills have died in committee due to a lack of sponsors. Congressional legislation is necessary for hibakusha to be covered for the uninsured costs of radiation-related illnesses because federal law exempts the United States "from paying claims arising from the 'lawful conduct of military activities in wartime.' "[11] Pragmatic in their expectations, American hibakusha have never asked for an apology from the government and have sought only modest assistance, not the kind of compensation that has been extended, in recent years, to atomic veterans and civilian victims of radiation exposure.[12]

The Nisei Experience

There are an estimated fifteen hundred American hibakusha, most of whom live in Hawaii or in the major cities of the West Coast. Forty percent of American hibakusha are either citizens or permanent residents of the United States as a result of international marriages, 20 percent immigrated to the United States after the war, and 40 percent are Nisei who were in Japan when the war began and were unable to return to the United States.

Nisei had strong cultural ties to Japan because of formative experiences in the home and through the religious and social institutions of the Japanese-American community, but they also shared the common experience of most immigrant groups. As the first generation to be born in the United States they had a certain ambivalence about their heritage and were willing to sacrifice those ties in an effort to fit into the larger American culture. In the 1930s and 1940s, however, Nisei had to contend with growing anti-Japanese prejudice, fueled by nativist groups, farmers, and businessmen who were threatened by the economic success of the Issei and Nisei. To escape their untenable position — too Americanized to be wholly Japanese, but knowing they could never be fully assimilated into American society — many talented Nisei returned to Japan. They joined those who were stranded in Japan because of complicated personal circumstances. Some were Kibei ("return to Japan") Nisei whose parents had sent them to Japan for education and employment opportunities (for the boys) and for marriage partners (for the girls).

The relatively large number of Nisei in Hiroshima in August 1945 — estimated to be 3,200[13] — was partially due to the fact that a high percentage of Issei had originated from Hiroshima Prefecture and many still had family ties to the area. Some Hiroshima residents thought the presence of the Nisei served to protect them. According to Kanji Kuramoto, "Hiroshima for a long time had no air raids. So some people were saying, maybe Americans don't want to raid because a lot of Nisei were living there."[14] The Nisei in Hiroshima were not a homogenous community, and their wartime experiences were as a diverse as their reasons for being there. Jane Iwashika's loneliness and isolation were exacerbated by the ill-treatment of teachers and authority figures.

> I wasn't happy in Japan. The teachers gave me a bad time because I wasn't a Japanese citizen. To them I was an alien, a ghost, I didn't exist. I was just a kid and I didn't care what Japan was doing. All I knew was that my mother, father, brothers, and sisters were in the United States so I secretly rooted for America. I didn't even know that they had been put in concentration camps. They were in Tule Lake. I was separated from them for a good ten years.[15]

Rinjiro Sodei found other Nisei who adapted to their environment and grew up to be military-minded young people.

> In fact, quite a few [learned] judo and kendo in the hope of some day triumphing over American soldiers.... Nisei who were in their teens when the war broke out had to make a more conscious effort to prove their loyalty to Japan.... While Japan was winning, Japanese could afford to feel some generosity toward the Nisei. However, when Japan began to lose, the "American-borns" began to be treated as spies. For this reason, they had to demonstrate "faithfulness to the Emperor and loyalty to the Nation." The fact that it was not unusual for these American-born youths to apply for the pilot training corps, the Naval Academy or the Military Academy clearly illustrates their predicament.[16]

Jack Dairiki, a Nisei who had gone to Japan with his father in August 1941, remembers being "caught in the middle":

> Our American-made radio was confiscated [by the Japanese police]. One of my [American-born] friends was jailed in his relatives' village. Whenever I saw a U.S. plane go over, inside myself I rooted for it.[17]

Frances Tomosawa, who had gone to Japan for three years of study, sums it up simply: "We were stranded in Japan. We weren't there to help Japan; we were stranded."[18]

Recalling their first reactions to the bomb, Japanese hibakusha remember "rage against the pilots, or the U.S. government, or the Japanese military men who were willing to sacrifice civilian lives," but American hibakusha report more complex and painful responses:

> Some say they were profoundly "embarrassed" because it was fellow Americans who dropped the bombs. Others felt childish hope: did this mean the war was over and they could go home now? And there was confusion, an emotion that persists in various forms to this day: "If my cousin is dead in front of me and I am burned in the face, and this is called a victory for America, does that mean I am the enemy?[19]

The loneliness, stress, and fears that the Nisei felt were complicated by the fact that many of them had dual citizenship. American citizens by virtue of being born in this country, they were Japanese citizens because their births were registered in the records of their paternal villages. Nisei who reached legal maturity during the war would automatically lose American citizenship if they served in the military or voted in a Japanese election. (Ironically some Nisei innocently voted in Japan's first post-war democratic election in a spirit of obedience to the Occupation.) Many Nisei were forcibly recruited to work in military or civil defense units in Japan. They responded to the challenge of proving their loyalty in ways that mirrored the response of their relatives living in the United States.

The *Nichi Bei*, an influential San Francisco Japanese-language newspaper, was forced to suspend publication on December 8, 1941, but it resumed operations three weeks later, with the poignant words of its editor:

> It is unfortunate that the U.S. and Japan are at war. We 100,000 Japanese in this country, despite our sincere hope for peace in the Pacific, can't help but feel deep concern. Until recently, we were good-natured inhabitants and parents of loyal second-generation citizens, but now suddenly we have to receive the treatment accorded the people of an enemy country. And for this, we cannot blame anyone.
>
> The generosity of the U.S. government, based on the principle of freedom and justice, has allowed us to issue the paper, despite the fact that we are aliens from an enemy country. [Author's note: They were aliens because the law would not allow them to be otherwise.]
>
> Needless to say, we have decided that this land is our permanent residence. We have lived peacefully and worked for our living under the protection of the laws of this country. Even though our physical appearance is that of Japanese, our minds have already been Americanized. We have sung for Americanism and praised democracy. In the future we Japanese in this country will naturally cooperate with the policy

of the U.S. government with all our effort, and we must make a vow that we will never act any way to harm our country and profit the enemy country.[20]

The Japanese-American community was divided over its response to internment and how best to prove loyalty to the country that had deemed them disloyal by virtue of their race.

> The Japanese are a proud people, and their concern for honor is a significant influence in guiding their personal behavior. ...Individual wrongdoing brought shame not just to the individual and his family but to the Japanese community, the Japanese nation, and all Japanese people. Perhaps that is why we had such mixed feelings of guilt and shame, as well as horror and anger, when Japan attacked Pearl Harbor.[21]

Two-thirds of the 110,000 internees were American-born Nisei, and 33,000 of them enlisted in the Nisei 442nd Combat Team and 100th Battalion; service in the European theater earned them the distinction of being the most decorated units in American military history. After the war these Nisei soldiers served in the Occupation forces in Japan. Other Nisei renounced their American citizenship and were repatriated to Japan in November 1945, joined by a group of about 2,000 Issei who refused to believe that Japan had been defeated.[22]

There were an estimated 15,000 Nisei living in Japan at the end of the war, of whom 10,000 were eligible to return to the United States. In February 1946, American military personnel began reviewing the cases of Nisei who had performed services for the Japanese government, and six months later the first Nisei returned to the United States; by 1948 there were roughly 5,000 returnees, almost 10 percent of whom were hibakusha.

Nisei returned to face the myriad personal decisions necessary after such wrenching turmoil and transition: the need to make decisions about where to live (even after the war, there were areas where prejudice against Japanese was translated into physical or economic hardship), marriage and family, career and education — tasks subsumed under the larger one of reintegration into American society. Men accomplished that task with greater ease because their work lives demanded a fluency in both language and customs. Nisei women more often assumed the traditional role of homemakers.

Kanji Kuramoto was born in Hawaii, and when he was four his mother took him to Japan to visit a sick grandfather, the first in what became a series of family illnesses that delayed their return to the United States until the war began. He finished high school in Hiroshima and in 1945 was studying engineering in Kyoto.

Kuramoto is a secondary hibakusha: he was not in Hiroshima on August 6 but managed to get on the first train going to the bombed city and arrived there on the night of August 8. He found his injured mother and brother in a crude shelter near the ruins of their home, but his father was missing. Kuramoto spent two weeks searching for his father, and although he never found him or his corpse, he received a considerable exposure to radiation. He saw and heard things that have never left him.

> People just sat there half-dead, yet their minds were clear. I had to help cremate bodies. I smelled the stench of burning bodies on my hands for years. I wanted to help survivors, but I couldn't....I could only give them water. People gave me their names and addresses and asked me to contact their families to let them know that they were alive. I wrote each name on a sheet of paper. I felt obligated to help. Oftentimes, I'd walk by a few minutes later and they'd be dead.[23]

Kanji Kuramoto's story is like that of other returned Nisei: "I tried to block my memories of the bomb because it was hell. I was young and still healthy. I didn't want to say anything bad about my country."[24] In 1969 he joined a few other American hibakusha in an informal friendship association, and two years later they formally organized CABS as an advocacy organization for American hibakusha. Fifty people responded to an ad that Kuramoto had placed, some of whom "had never spoken to anyone, not even their own families, about being hibakusha. In the seventies they still feared ridicule, rejection, and the strong anti-Japanese sentiment left over from World War II."[25] Kuramato presided over CABS until 1992 and helped establish active CABS chapters in Los Angeles, San Francisco, and Seattle.

Doubly Rebuffed

In 1981 a support group, Friends of Hibakusha (FOH) formed to assist the survivors. FOH publishes a quarterly newsletter, *The Paper Crane,* provides fundraising and coordinating support for the visits of Japanese physicians, and plays an important role in education and publicity.

In 1988 FOH began an ambitious oral history project; the taped and transcribed interviews with American hibakusha will eventually be housed at the library of the University of California at Berkeley and with the Japanese-American Historical Society. While respecting the need of hibakusha "to weigh their desire for privacy and anonymity against an equal desire for public understanding and needed medical programs," the organizers of the project hope that "the telling of their personal stories will help sensitize policy makers to the survivors' needs, as well as bring their messages of peace to more people."[26]

Since 1977 Japanese physicians have made biennial visits to the United States, and on each visit more and more American hibakusha have taken advantage of the opportunity to be evaluated by people who are knowledgeable about the delayed health effects of radiation. The visits of the medical teams, sponsored by the Japanese government and the Hiroshima Medical Association, are an expression of caring that ameliorates the excessive isolation of American hibakusha. One Japanese physician noticed that "hibakusha here [in the United States] suffer more emotional and psychological anxiety, partly because of the lack of sophisticated medical facilities. Therefore, we emphasize psychological treatment and support in addition to the extensive medical exams."[27]

> I've had anemia for ten years. I used to have stomach aches, and I had to have some shots. Ten years after returning to the U.S., I fainted and was hospitalized.... My doctor used to say to me, "Eat more meat." In July of 1952 I had a baby. I was so anxious, wondering if my baby would have arms and legs, would the baby be healthy. I was always wondering. That's why, just after she was born, I counted her toes and fingers. I was relieved because she was fine.[28]

> Before the bomb, I was really healthy. Since then, it's been really up and down. Right after the bomb I had malnutrition. ...In 1957, I was in the hospital for seven months. In 1979, they found cancer in my uterus so I had a hysterectomy. Then they found cancer in my stomach so they gave me radiation treatments. I was in the hospital for a year.[29]

The Atomic Bomb Casualty Commission (ABCC) drew its research population from the 1950 Japanese census; by that date, most American hibakusha had returned to the United States. It was not until 1974 that an effort was made to determine the radiation exposure of American hibakusha. The project was organized by the Oak Ridge National Laboratory; CABS located American hibakusha; and the actual interviews were conducted by Hiroaki Yamada, an ABCC epidemiologist. Yamada interviewed over three hundred people, many of whom used the opportunity to narrate not only the details of their bomb experience — how far they were from ground zero, whether they were shielded by wood or concrete, if they were exposed to "black rain" — but to express their long-suppressed feelings and fears. Yamada the scientist was forced

to act as "part Buddhist priest, part psychiatrist,"[30] but those sub-
jective findings never entered his final assessment of radiation dose
levels.

There is a complicated relationship between Japan and its emigrants to the United States. The first emigrants (1868) were
contract agricultural workers recruited for three-year periods on
Hawaiian sugar plantations. They came to the United States largely
for economic reasons. Needing funds in its efforts to modernize
Japan, the government of Emperor Meiji instituted a harsh tax
structure at a time of economic depression, forcing many farmers into bankruptcy. Emigrants seized the opportunity to save
money, return to Japan to pay off their debts, and resume farming.
They thought of themselves as temporary sojourners, not potential
immigrants.

> The Meiji Restoration had unified the country, and the new
> state was able to regulate emigration. Driven by a rising
> nationalism, the government viewed overseas Japanese as
> representatives of their homeland and required prospective
> emigrants to apply for permission to leave for Hawaii and the
> United States. Review boards screened them to ensure that
> they were healthy and literate and would creditably "main-
> tain Japan's national honor." The Japanese government had
> received reports on the conditions of the Chinese in Amer-
> ica and was determined to monitor carefully the quality of its
> emigrants.[31]

There were harsh living and working conditions on the plantations, but a policy of rigidly segregating camps on the basis of
worker nationality allowed the Japanese emigrants to maintain
strong cultural ties. Some emigrants chose to delay their return
to Japan in order to seek higher paid work on the mainland.
The passage of the Chinese Exclusion Act of 1882 had resulted
in a shortage of low-paid workers in fishing, logging, and railroad construction; the Japanese, with their reputation for being
diligent employees, were frequently hired for these positions. Their
numbers increased rapidly in the 1920s and 1930s.

Many Japanese turned to agriculture, work that they were familiar with and that did not require fluency in either language
or cultural mores. Although hampered by their relative poverty,
they were able to progress from being common laborers to owners
of small truck farms through creative leasing and sharecropping
arrangements. Issei in urban areas were able to support a web
of small family businesses (laundries, restaurants, grocery stores,
boarding houses) to meet the needs of other immigrants. In the

first decade of the 1900s the Issei began to marry, often sending to Japan for picture brides.

Ironically, the very success of the farmers and small business owners resulted in a new round of anti-Japanese legislation. In 1913 the California legislature passed the Alien Land Act, which made aliens ineligible for the ownership of agricultural lands. The attorney general of California put it frankly: "The fundamental basis of all legislation has been, and is, race undesirability."[32] Other discriminatory legislation followed: in 1906, Oriental students were segregated out of San Francisco schools. The Japanese government protested, and President Theodore Roosevelt intervened. Roosevelt was anxious to mollify a Japan that was emerging as a world power after its decisive victory in the Russo-Japanese War. The negotiated settlement ended segregated schooling, in exchange for which Japan agreed to self-imposed quotas on passports, limiting them to family members of those already in the United States.

The Immigration Quota Act, which Congress passed in 1924, limited immigration from each country to 2 percent of the number of immigrants from that country who were living in the United States in 1890. The Japanese, as aliens ineligible for citizenship because of their race, were denied entry, and although the Japanese government protested the legislation, they received no response from the United States.

Given the precedent of the involvement of the Japanese national government in matters relating to Japanese Americans, it is not surprising that American hibakusha would turn to Japan for assistance when they were rebuffed by the United States. In 1967, a visiting American hibakusha met informally with Hiroshima city officials to request that radiation specialists be sent to the United States. In 1968, a delegation of twenty American hibakusha met with Hiroshima mayor Setsuo Yamada, who, although sympathetic, cited financial constraints and legal limitations on foreign physicians seeing patients in the United States for his inability to help.[33] In 1971, an American hibakusha appeared on Japanese television to talk about their plight; the public's emotional response to her plea probably had much to do with the willingness of the city of Hiroshima to sponsor an August 1972 visit by a public health expert, Hiroshi Maki, M.D. Dr. Maki examined forty-three hibakusha during his four-day stay in San Francisco. Sodei's language in describing this visit is revealing of Japanese attitudes toward Nisei:

> *On this day the hibakusha behaved admirably like real Japanese.* In the presence of a doctor from Hiroshima, they

were to receive a real physical examination. Their expectations were high, in contrast to the past when their cases were
not understood by American doctors. But beyond that, *they
tried hard to prove that they were worthy of being helped.*
... [Upon his return to Hiroshima, Dr. Maki reported that]
"there was not a single patient who would qualify under
Japan's A-Bomb Medical Care Law, except a lady who had
a neurological problem."[34] (emphasis added)

One of the difficulties in trying to assess the health effects of
radiation is how to measure the impact of anxiety. Various illnesses have become manifest in the years since the bombing, and
the uncertainty of what diseases will be shown to correlate with
radiation in the future is greatly unsettling to hibakusha. American
hibakusha can have difficulty communicating with their physicians,
in part because of language difficulties, but also because those
American and Japanese-American physicians are unfamiliar with
the nuances of radiation-related illnesses. The Hiroshima physicians are better able to ameliorate the anxiety felt by American
hibakusha, particularly as they age. Early visits of the medical
teams found relatively few American hibakusha with diseases for
which a health allowance would be paid, but, because of the increase in the number and mean age of those examined, at the 1989
visit 30 percent of hibakusha suffered from an illness that would
be eligible for the allowance.

In the 1920s, the Issei and Nisei communities turned to Japan
with the expectation that it would intercede with the United
States government over its discriminatory immigration policies.
They were disappointed to find that "Japanese officials were more
concerned with the state of Japan's political and economic relations with the United States than they were with the well-being
of its mostly laboring-class emigrants."[35] American hibakusha encountered the same treatment forty years later when they futilely
appealed to "shared blood ties" in their petition to Japan for help
in arranging a medical visit.

The vice-consul responded, in the perfunctory manner typical
of government officials, that nothing could be done in California; that the memories of Pearl Harbor, revived every year
on December 7, kept latent hostilities alive; and that the visitors should try the Japanese Embassy in Washington, D.C.
The visitors then asked in what manner and format a petition
to the Japanese Ambassador should be prepared, but the vice-
consul did not answer. Throughout the 30-minute interview,
this minor official sat with both feet resting on the coffee ta-
ble. Okai and Simoda [the two American hibakusha] felt deep

anger and chagrin at such treatment, which went far beyond any superficial show of discourtesy and lack of consideration. Ever since the Meiji period, Japanese overseas officials had shown contempt toward Japanese immigrants. Possibly this custom had been inherited by their post-war counterparts. Or could it have been that this official took the two visitors for troublemakers who were reminders of the thorny problem that the atomic bombing poses to U.S.-Japan relations? The two visitors read such overtones into the attitude of this official.

The U.S. government was undependable and when the Japanese government, with whom they shared blood ties, treated them so insolently, they felt as if they had been thrown into an abyss between the two countries.[36]

The appeal to blood ties and the expectation that Japan would be of help to them have been constant themes in the narrative of American hibakusha. Rebuffed by the United States government, which has continued to repeat its claim that it owes nothing to American hibakusha, they turn to Japan only to be rebuffed again, a continual alteration of hopes that *this* time their pleas for care will be heard, only to be rudely dismissed and reminded once again of their essential, profound homelessness. This isolation and sense of abandonment is exacerbated by their perception that no one listens to their feelings or makes any effort to understand their situation.

Korean Hibakusha

It is revealing to contrast the attitudes and action of American and Korean hibakusha. There were an estimated two million Koreans in Japan at the end of the war, many of whom had been brought to Japan as forced labor in the years after the 1910 annexation of Korea.[37] Japan imposed a numbingly harsh occupation on the Koreans, confiscating their land and natural resources, and forcing them to change their names, religion, and language. "All Korean A-bomb victims — whether voluntary or involuntary immigrants — are distinguished from Japanese victims in that they were long victims of repressive policies before falling victim to the atomic bombs."[38]

I find it difficult to talk about a good part of my life. Being Korean, I cannot divorce myself from the suffering of my compatriots, and I am ripped apart by my memories. Because of Japanese militarism, I was pushed into forced labor and

made to suffer countless instances of discrimination and op-
pression, finally becoming a victim of the atomic bomb. Fate
decreed that I be coerced into sacrificing my body and blood
"for the sake of the Emperor."[39]

The author of the above passage recounts his rage at the lack of
treatment and respect accorded dying Korean victims of the bomb,
and he challenges the Japanese officials who ignored their pain:
"What do you intend to do? You are the ones who brought these
people to Japan against their will." He felt "a sudden exhilara-
tion" and "bewildered happiness" when hearing of Japan's defeat,
but then,

> I told myself that for every Korean killed, hundreds of Japa-
> nese must have died — old people, women, and children, all
> non-combatants, all slaughtered. Nor was there any differ-
> ence in the pain and sadness of those who lost people close
> to them or who suffered injury. Who bears the burden of re-
> sponsibility for the indiscriminate slaughter of the pawns of
> Japanese imperialism? America, are you satisfied now?[40]

The lives of Korean hibakusha have been characterized by a
desperate, harsh poverty, scant medical care, and the same discrimination that has afflicted hibakusha in Japan and the United
States. Their plight is exacerbated by the fact that South Korea lost
the right to press Japan for compensation for atomic bomb damages in the 1965 treaty that normalized relations between the two
countries.

It was not until 1968 that a memorial service for Korean victims
of the bomb was held in Hiroshima. Some have noted that the most
eloquent testimony to the shameful treatment of Korean hibakusha
remains the fact that the monument to their victims is located outside the confines of Hiroshima's Peace Memorial Park, but this is
partially due to differences within the Korean community. "Koreans loyal to South Korea and those loyal to North Korea wanted
to erect separate monuments in the Peace Park; Hiroshima City
refused, as Korea was not divided in August 1945 and the City
wanted to stay out of post-war political hostilities among Koreans.
South-oriented Koreans put up their monument on the outside.
The City continues discussions on a 'unified' Korean monument
within the Park."[41]

Korean hibakusha have long understood what a Japanese court
ruled in 1976, that "although the atomic bomb was dropped by
the United States, Japan began the war which led to its use. The
victims are not to be held responsible. Under the law of National
Indemnities, the aid to the victims is to be the responsibility of the
government of Japan."[42]

The political perceptions of Korean hibakusha shaped what was essentially a campaign of civil disobedience to obtain medical care. Where American hibakusha appealed for consideration, Korean hibakusha demanded, not with words, but with actions. In the late 1960s and early 1970s individual Koreans went to Japan to seek medical care and request a Hibakusha Health Book. Some went to Japan legally, their visas indicating that they were there to obtain medical treatment for bomb-related illnesses; others were there illegally, and by their very presence they challenged the assumption that only permanent residents of Japan were eligible for hibakusha aid.

The most significant case of a Korean hibakusha was that of Son Jin-Dou, who was arrested in December 1970, having entered Japan illegally to obtain treatment for an atomic bomb–related disease. The following June he was sentenced to ten months in jail. The *Chugoku Shimbun* reported that, on hearing the sentence, he "declared accusatively, 'You should think about who caused my misery in the first place.' " Son continued his appeals and in a landmark decision in March 1978 won the right to receive a Hibakusha Health Book, paving the way for the passage of a broader hibakusha relief bill. Eligible American hibakusha are entitled to receive care in Japan, but as a practical matter few people can afford the transportation costs such trips would entail.[43]

In 1971 Korean hibakusha received their first visit from a Japanese medical team, six years before the first team came to the United States. In December 1973 a medical center for hibakusha was opened in Hypochon, South Korea; located in an area where an estimated three thousand hibakusha lived, the center was funded by the National Council for Peace and Against Nuclear Weapons so that "greater pressure would be placed on the Japanese government to acknowledge and provide relief for the Korean hibakusha."[44]

Invisible Outsiders

American hibakusha, with a more amorphous relationship with both the Japanese and American governments, have been hampered in their ability to communicate the complexities of the issues their community faces. The myth that they are Japanese citizens is held even at the highest levels of the United States government. In 1978, when Kanji Kuramoto wrote to President Jimmy Carter requesting assistance in expediting the visits of the Japanese medical teams, his letter was forwarded to and answered by the chief of the Japan desk at the State Department.

CABS has been forced to adopt a politically moderate and cautious stance, careful not to exacerbate members' fears that they will be seen as the wartime enemy, because this opens up the terrible prospect of having their loyalty suspected again. CABS has had to appease a wide variety of supporters, from the Japanese physicians and officials involved with the medical visits to some of its own politically conservative members.

Kuramoto tried to lessen the isolation of American hibakusha through his active involvement with the National Association of Radiation Survivors (NARS), an educational and advocacy group for atomic veterans and their widows, "downwinders" (those whose farms and livestock were affected by atmospheric nuclear tests), workers in nuclear power plants, and Navajo uranium miners. He was heartened by their successful lobbying for compensation: in 1988 Congress passed the Radiation-Exposed Veterans Compensation Act, to compensate veterans who had been in Hiroshima or Nagasaki during the Occupation or who were exposed to radiation as part of atmospheric nuclear testing. Two years later similar legislation was passed to compensate other victims of radiation, notably downwinders and uranium miners.

Kuramoto approached Congressional staffers with a request that the 1990 legislation include hibakusha. "They laughed at me. They were openly hostile toward me. They said they wouldn't even think about jeopardizing the bill. They said there was an attendant political risk to adding hibakusha onto the bill because they were a part of an enemy nation at the time of the bombing."[45]

The American hibakusha desire to speak has been frustrated by an equal, if not greater, fear of being used by political groups, and so being vulnerable to charges of disloyalty. Pressure was put on CABS leaders in 1976 when the California electorate debated Proposition 15, a ballot initiative concerning the safety of nuclear power plants, which was supported by environmental and peace groups and opposed by state utilities and labor unions. Kuramoto received anonymous calls from the bill's opponents, who promised CABS financial assistance if they would join the opposition; it would certainly have been a psychological coup if victims of an atomic attack had endorsed nuclear power plants. Peace and environmental groups, unable to offer money, did promise active support for the hibakusha medical bill then pending in the California legislature. "For hibakusha, who wanted to just live quietly in the United States, it was a major effort to ask for passage of a medical aid bill. To join a political group and thereby become the object of the anger and hatred of the opposing group was much more than the organization could endure.... Strict neutrality was the only way the weak organization could survive."[46] Despite

Kuramoto's personal sympathies with the bill's supporters, CABS maintained its strict neutrality and silence.

Some American hibakusha spoke at Nuclear Freeze rallies in the 1980s, but according to filmmaker Steven Okazaki, "Organizers wanted to get people on stage who had the most scars and who had experienced the most emotional suffering. It was hard enough for them having to tell their stories to large groups of strangers, but it was equally as painful to have their high expectations dashed when political activists got tired of the issue and moved on to another cause. Many hibakusha felt used."[47]

The tepid support that the Japanese American Citizens League (JACL) has offered to hibakusha is indicative of the ambivalence of the larger Japanese-American community. (One notable exception to this rule was the late Dr. Thomas Noguchi, longtime Los Angeles County coroner, who began offering American hibakusha his intelligent and sustained guidance in the early 1970s.) The JACL has provided some lobbying assistance from its office in Washington, D.C., but the needs of American hibakusha have never been high on its agenda. Quite possibly it was fear of reopening the emotions of the wartime years and not simply gratuitous insults that led them to provide the following direction to CABS in 1975, when the late Emperor Hirohito visited the United States: "While the Emperor is visiting the U.S., the Atomic Bomb Survivors Association shall not conduct any activity. Furthermore, they should refrain from welcoming the Emperor in the name of CABS."[48]

American hibakusha living in Hawaii are less inclined to be activists, despite the large numbers of Japanese Americans — and their consequently greater political influence — on the islands.

> The Japanese in Hawaii had become assimilated in a way very different from that of their countrymen on the mainland. Far from being a small scattered minority in a vast land, they were a numerically dominant group in a multiethnic society. Furthermore, the Japanese in Hawaii lived in a more racially tolerant culture and were geographically closer to Japan, which made homeland influences stronger. Although their early history was marked by discrimination similar to that faced by Japanese on the West Coast, the Hawaiian Japanese after World War II enjoyed a good deal of success and political power.[49]

Even before 1959, when Hiroshima and Honolulu became sister cities, Hawaiian Japanese Americans had raised several hundred thousand dollars for relief of hibakusha. Hawaiian hibakusha have been relatively passive in supporting CABS. Organizers were sur-

prised by the reluctance of Hawaiian hibakusha to participate in
Dr. Yamada's 1974 research trip. Dr. Harada reflected:

> Since people living in Hawaii are warm-hearted and very
> loyal towards the United States, they might have been prone
> to overcome and forget the atomic bomb experience as being
> irrelevant, and not worth unearthing at this point.... In this
> environment it might have been their sincere inclination to
> "let sleeping dogs lie...." On the mainland, a U.S. hibaku-
> sha's struggle begins with the need to strive for recognition of
> his American identity by other Americans, whereas in Hawaii
> hibakusha do not need to.[50]

In 1974 legislation was introduced in the California state legislature that would have established an Institute for Research
and Treatment for Nuclear Radiation whose purpose was to offer free treatment to radiation victims. The bill's language totally
avoided any mention of Hiroshima and Nagasaki and offered
similar care to workers at nuclear power plants. Sponsors hoped
that the development of a center, staffed by people knowledgeable
about radiation-related illnesses, would help provide reassurance
for hibakusha. Unfortunately, the University of California, whose
medical school was to be the site of the proposed center, publicly
opposed the plan, arguing that it was the responsibility of the federal rather than state government to care for hibakusha. The bill
was later amended to allow hibakusha eligibility under California's
medical assistance program, Medi-Cal. The incomes of most American hibakusha, however, are higher than the program's eligibility
guidelines. Moreover, Japanese Americans avoid dependence on
social welfare programs because their traditional ethos considers
it shameful to receive such aid.

Japanese and Korean hibakusha have evolved an actual and
symbolic language of witness by their direct, clear protest and have
used that protest as a symbolic way of giving meaning to their
survival. Despite the risk that their symbolic speech would be mis-
understood, despite knowing that they could and have been used
by others, they have developed a response to the bomb that is
seasoned by political maturity. American hibakusha have been unable to do this, in part because of their inability to form alliances
with the peace and anti-nuclear movements that would offset their
scant numbers and lack of political sophistication. These would be
formidable constraints for any group to overcome, let alone relatively older Japanese Americans who carry the additional burdens
of bomb-related illnesses and anxiety about their health.

> There are lots of radical parties in Japan that use Hiroshima,
> not for peace, but for criticizing America. These peace groups

come and try to cooperate with us, and use us sometimes. I get very disturbed when they complain about the American government, so I try not to get involved. We don't want to be used as a political symbol. We're not for or against anything. All we can say is that we've experienced an atomic bomb, and we think it's terribly dangerous. But we don't want to take any political stand.[51]

Opposition to nuclear weapons is a political stand, but American hibakusha have been unable to be overtly political. Their strategy has been to emphasize the goodness of the American people and express the hope that the larger society will become aware of the responsibility for addressing the injustices that resulted from the government's use of the atomic bomb against its own citizens. This has been a futile argument because most Americans are unwilling to engage questions about the use of the bomb. Their appeal to American goodness is a reflection of *amae,* but it is also perhaps the only strategy they could have adopted, given their isolation and lack of power. American hibakusha have tried to resolve an American situation with a Japanese solution, but they are double outsiders — as hibakusha and as American hibakusha — so it is no wonder that they have been rendered invisible.

But away from the glare of publicity and power, American hibakusha have shaped an impressive witness because with their very lives they rebuke those who would argue for the primacy of loyalty. In their quiet struggles, American hibakusha illuminate the unworthiness of the nation state that demands obedience from its citizens but returns neither protection nor compassion. Theirs is a story rife with irony, but none more so than the fact that these people, intensely loyal to two nations and cultures, can find no sustenance from either.

5

The Mystic of Nagasaki

TAKASHI NAGAI, M.D.

— ♋ —

Walking with God through Urakami's nuclear wasteland has taught
me the depths of His friendship.

— Takashi Nagai, M.D.

On Thursday, August 9, 1945, at 11:02 A.M. the B-29 *Bock's Car*
released a plutonium-fueled atomic bomb from its flying altitude of
29,000 feet. The bomb burst 500 meters from the Urakami Cathedral, in the valley that was home to 15,000 of Nagasaki's 20,000
Catholics; of these 10,000 died,[1] a significant portion of the bomb's
79,000 immediate victims. Six days later Emperor Hirohito accepted the terms of the Potsdam Declaration, ending fifteen years
of war in the Pacific.

The names of Hiroshima and Nagasaki are yoked together,
but there are significant differences between them. The Hiroshima
bomb was fueled by uranium while that used at Nagasaki was a
more powerful plutonium weapon. Hiroshima — a flat city surrounded by mountains on three sides — suffered comparatively
greater damage because the bomb was detonated over the city center, and the subsequent firestorms destroyed a great percentage
of its physical structures. In contrast the hypocenter in Nagasaki
was a hilly suburb in the northern part of the city and the damage was more localized; "over one third of all buildings were
severely damaged,"[2] and "total destruction extended 2 kilometers
in every direction."[3] The extent of destruction had a profound effect on the relationships between the hibakusha and non-hibakusha
populations of the two cities.

Everyone in Hiroshima at the time of the bomb felt exposed
to it, and was later designated as hibakusha. Each of them
encountered two types of outsiders: returning Hiroshima residents who happened to be elsewhere when the bomb fell,
outsiders only in the sense of being non-hibakusha; and those

with no previous connection to the city who decided to move there from former overseas possessions or from other parts of Japan. Nagasaki hibakusha, in contrast, were from the beginning a minority in relationship to non-hibakusha residents of their city. Since there was no comparable influx of people from the outside...they have tended to be absorbed by the original non-hibakusha population. They have therefore never experienced the Hiroshima hibakusha's sense of being dispossessed by an amorphous mass of outsiders who without having suffered reaped later rewards. This threat to identity could well have been a further stimulus for Hiroshima survivors to reiterate the importance of their A-bomb exposure, since the focus upon it, however painful, was a way of avoiding a sense of being snuffed out entirely.[4]

Nagasaki has been the neglected atomic city. One of Lifton's informants noted, with "atomic bomb gallows humor," that Nagasaki is "like the man who flew the Atlantic after Lindbergh."[5] But that neglect may have given the city the necessary privacy with which to explore its A-bomb experience. Outsiders bring a different intensity to their demands on Hiroshima and Nagasaki. Nagasaki has, to some extent, been spared the burden of the intense scrutiny and symbolic imagery foisted on Hiroshima by the press and peace activists, partly due to their respective distances from Tokyo.

Nagasaki had a stronger pre-war historical identity to draw on when it began to rebuild. Nagasaki was well known in the West because it had been the port of entrance for European traders and missionaries. Hiroshima was an important regional army center but few people outside of Japan knew the city. The center of Japanese Catholicism, Nagasaki knew a brutal history of martyrdom and persecution, and this led in turn to an atmosphere of conservatism and caution. Contributing to that ethos was the city's major economic force, the Mitsubishi Corporation, founded in 1870. Mitsubishi's munitions factories and shipbuilding prospered during the 1930s, under Japan's expansionist policies. "Dedication of the major industries in Nagasaki to armaments production brought with it the militarization of the social and cultural life of the citizens, whose rights were suppressed and who in the prevailing war hysteria were politically silenced."[6]

There were many non-Japanese living in Nagasaki in August 1945: several thousand conscripted Korean laborers, 600 Chinese merchants (there had been significant trade between Shanghai and Nagasaki), 650 Taiwanese employed in Japan (Taiwan was then a Japanese colony), and an estimated 350 prisoners of war, mostly Dutch, Australian, and British, imprisoned in two camps.[7]

Even those who justify the use of the Hiroshima atomic bomb as a military necessity find it difficult to ascribe the same motivation to the Nagasaki bomb. It was, instead, an act of gratuitous cruelty intended to make a political statement to the Soviet Union. "Since responsibility for timing the A-bomb sorties was delegated to the bomber command on Tinian Island, Washington never scheduled a pause to monitor the Japanese response to the first assault and the entry of the USSR into the war."[8]

The differences between the two atomic-bombed cities have been capsulized in the succinct if inaccurate phrase, "the rage of Hiroshima and the prayers of Nagasaki." It is tempting to see the cities as neatly symmetrical opposites, and in fact, some journalists have compared the "good" city of Nagasaki (which has chosen to forget its past tragedies) with the more strident (ideological) incantations of Hiroshima, which has been accused of "enshrining" its atomic scars, a caricature that may be comforting to observers disturbed by Hiroshima's aggressive portrayal of the bomb.

Hiroshima city officials labeled as libelous a 1962 article in an American news magazine that contrasted Hiroshima — "its chilling museum of atomic horrors has been massively and masochistically documented," "has made an industry of its fate...the only city in the world that advertises its past history" — with Nagasaki, where citizens were "less fearful of 'atom sickness,' markedly gayer and more relaxed" and concluded that "Hiroshima has remained a stark symbol of man's inhumanity to man; Nagasaki is a monument to forgiveness." The simplistic dichotomy of that article still colors public perceptions of the two cities: "Hiroshima today is grimly obsessed by that long-ago mushroom cloud; Nagasaki lives resolutely in the present."[9]

The person primarily responsible for articulating "the prayers of Nagasaki" was Takashi Nagai, M.D. (1908–51). Dr. Nagai is the Nagasaki counterpart of Hiroshima's Mayor Hamai, and this first and most important post-bomb spokesman drew on the imagery and self-knowledge of the city's long history of martyrdom.

A Catholic convert, Dr. Nagai was a physician by training but his nature was that of a deeply prayerful man whose contemplative vision allowed him to stand in the ruins of Nagasaki and proclaim, "The Lord has given: the Lord has taken away. Blessed be the name of the Lord!" "Let us give thanks that Nagasaki was chosen for the sacrifice. Let us give thanks that through this sacrifice peace was given to the world and freedom of religion to Japan."[10] Jesuit Father William Johnston, the English translator of Nagai's most popular work, *The Bells of Nagasaki,* calls the doctor "a mystic of peace for our time," the exemplar of an authentic religion that transcends rigid dogmas.[11]

Dr. Nagai represented the spiritual and theological milieu of pre-Vatican II Nagasaki, a community that, even today, remains the most conservative segment of the Japanese church. Other Japanese Catholics find it difficult to understand what one priest calls the "crucifixion mentality" of Nagasaki Catholics, a mentality rooted more in the early experience of martyrdom than the experience of the atomic bomb.[12] In 1981 when Pope John Paul II became the first pontiff to visit Hiroshima and Nagasaki, he seemed to obliquely criticize Dr. Nagai's spirituality with his clear denunciation that "war is an act of man, not God." The pope's visit, described by the *Chugoku Shimbun* as the most important visit of a church dignitary since St. Francis Xavier landed in Japan in 1549, led some Nagasaki hibakusha to ameliorate their stance of passive acceptance and become more actively involved with hibakusha and peace groups. One does not have accept Dr. Nagai's understanding of the bomb — "We had to obtain God's pardon through the offering of a great sacrifice" — to appreciate the spiritual courage that sought to find God's providential care in the very midst of the atomic desert.

> We Japanese, a vanquished people, must now walk along a path that is full of pain and suffering. The reparations imposed by the Potsdam Declaration are a heavy burden. But this painful path along which we walk carrying our burden — is it not also the path of hope which gives to us sinners an opportunity to expiate our sins?
>
> "Blessed are those who mourn for they shall be comforted." We must walk this way of expiation faithfully and sincerely. And as we walk in hunger and thirst, ridiculed, penalized, scourged, pouring with sweat and covered with blood, let us remember how Jesus Christ carried His cross to the hill of Calvary. He will give us courage.[13]

Nagasaki Catholics did not believe it was accidental that the war ended on August 15, a day they celebrate as the Feast of the Assumption of the Blessed Mother, under whose protection the Urakami Cathedral had been built. It is also the day on which they commemorate the 1549 arrival of St. Francis Xavier, the great Jesuit priest whose short three-year missionary effort led to the nucleus of a small but devout Christian community. "The missionaries taught them profoundest reverence for the majesty of God, a resolute shunning of sin, a high esteem for the Redemption, and a fervent love for the crucified Savior."[14] The faith of these Japanese Christians would be tested by years of persecution and more

than two centuries in hiding, but St. Francis Xavier judged them
correctly when he wrote to St. Ignatius of Loyola that "this Japanese people is the only one which seems to me likely to maintain
unshaken the Christian Faith, if once it has embraced it."[15]

The Christian population had reached an estimated two hundred thousand when the persecutions began in 1597. Japan's feudal
rulers perceived Christianity as intricately bound up with European
colonialism, but domestic political tensions and fear of foreign in-
vaders were not the only cause of resistance to Christianity. Some
missionaries themselves engendered hatred with methods that included wholesale baptisms and the destruction of Buddhist and
Shinto shrines in feudal states controlled by Christian lords.[16] In
1597 a "Spanish sea captain, rescued off the coast of Shikoku,
boasted that Christian missionaries were being used to soften up
Japan for an invasion by Western powers. When the Shogun of
Kyoto [Toyotomi Hideyoshi] heard this he had 7 missionaries and
17 of the flock arrested for being Christians."[17]

Condemned to death by crucifixion, the twenty-four, plus two
catechists, were forced to march five hundred miles from Osaka
to Nagasaki, where they were lashed to crosses on Nishizaka
Hill. Their deaths were witnessed by thousands of their fellow
Christians, who sang hymns and proclaimed their litany of belief. They died with words of pardon on their lips for the samurai
executioners who pierced their sides with swords.[18]

"After the Tokugawa unification of Japan in 1603, all other
cities except Kyoto were governed by politically decentralized feudal lords, but Nagasaki was controlled directly by the Tokugawa
shogunate in Tokyo, which cruelly persecuted the city's Catholic
population."[19] A law banning Catholic missionaries was passed in
1614; in 1623 Spanish and Portuguese traders were deported, although the latter were allowed to continue their trade until 1638.
After the Shimabara uprising (1637–38) in which forty thousand
peasants were killed in a rebellion against the feudal lords, the
Portuguese were forced to leave. The Dutch and Chinese were allowed to trade from Nagasaki, but the Dutch were confined to
Deshima, a small island in Nagasaki Bay. During the years of exclusion, 1636–1854, Japan's limited foreign contacts came through
Nagasaki.

From 1619 to 1858, when it was abolished as part of a treaty
with France, the shogunate enforced an annual New Year's event
when Christians were obliged to tread on *efumi*, plaques depicting
Jesus and/or Mary.

Most refused, whereupon they were seized, bound and hung
upside down over pits filled with reeking offal and left either

to apostatize or die. A small hole was bored into their fore-
heads so that death would not come too swiftly, and to
provide longer time for them to renounce their faith (the
Shogunate well understood the regenerative power and significance of martyrdom). Some were tortured with boiling water
from the hot springs at Unzen, while others were hung on
crosses erected by the sea; death came inch by inch on the
rising tide.[20]

By the middle of the seventeenth century it appeared as if
Christianity had disappeared from Japan. In fact, the Christian
community had gone underground and established complex structures — including "water people" to baptize and "calendar people"
to remember important liturgical events — that enabled them to
pass on their faith during 250 years when they were denied access
to the sacramental life and teaching authority of the Church.[21]

> They had survived the persecutions through geographic iso-
> lation and worshipping in secret. Although the rituals they
> followed varied somewhat from village to village, overall they
> were surprisingly similar.... These communities had evolved
> a hierarchical structure to serve their religious needs.[22]

Japan's isolation began to end after Commodore Matthew Perry
landed in Tokyo Bay in 1854 and demanded American trading
privileges. Other Western nations followed suit, and gradually, before the 1868 Meiji Restoration, foreigners were allowed to live in
and trade from Nagasaki, Yokohama, and Hakodate, and priests
were allowed to minister to the European community.

Father Bernard Petitjean, a missionary with the Paris Foreign
Mission Society (MEP), arrived in Japan in 1860 as the chaplain
for the French community in Nagasaki. He labored for five years
to construct a church that was dedicated to the twenty-six Martyrs
of Nagasaki. On March 17, 1865, a small group of Japanese Catholics (twelve to fifteen men, women, and children) went to that
church and with great trepidation asked Father Petitjean the questions that accorded with their legends, of "the return of the priests
in black ships, who would be known by their celibacy, their devotion to Mary, and their acknowledgement of the supremacy of
Rome."[23] Each generation of Hidden Christians had been taught
the three questions to determine the authenticity of a priest: Where
is [the statue of] Santa Maria? Are you married? Do you follow the
pope in Rome? When a stunned Father Petitjean answered them af-
firmatively they whispered their eloquent response, "The hearts of
all here are the same as yours."

In 1865 there were an estimated fifty thousand Hidden Christians in the villages of the Urakami Valley, north of Nagasaki, and in the remote Goto Islands.

> The doctrinally and politically passive Catholic community came into the open once again, accepting the lead of politically conservative and colonial-minded secular priests assigned from China and Indochina to Japan by the Paris Foreign Mission Society.... *In order to avoid calling attention to themselves, even after religious persecution had partially abated, the Catholics refused to question state policies.*[24] (emphasis added)

Approximately ten thousand Hidden Christians refused to rejoin the Catholic Church. Their descendants, who even today remain hidden, adhere to Catholic doctrine, but have evolved structures, including lay ministry and lay bishops, that make it unlikely that they will ever reaffiliate with Rome. Easter (the Rising Day) is the most important day of their church year. They baptize, make use of the Lord's Prayer and Apostle's Creed, and say a modified form of the rosary, but have no eucharistic ritual.

> These Hidden Christians maintain a deep loyalty to Francis Xavier, their first Christian missionary, and it is not equalled by any other loyalty.... They do not know, nor seek to know, of other Hidden Christians or Christian groups, except incidentally. There is no broad awareness of one another's needs from island to island, nor from village to village; nor is there a feeling of necessity to extend fellowship to others outside of the intimate family or church circle. Yet within their own families they have aggressively kept the faith.[25]

The majority of the Hidden Christians did return to the Roman Church, but acknowledgment of their faith initiated another six years of persecution (1867 to 1873), during which thousands of Catholics were exiled from their homes and suffered imprisonment and torture. Thirty-four hundred Urakami Christians were sent to nineteen prison camps, widely scattered throughout Japan. The experiences of the Moriyama family, hereditary leaders, were typical: the parents died in separate prisons, and Jinzaburo, their son, was tortured by "being plunged through the ice of a frozen pond, held under with hooked poles and fished out just in time to stay alive." When Jinzaburo failed to recant, his fourteen-year-old brother Yujiro became the victim:

> ... stripped and whipped mercilessly. He groaned in pain but held out. He was tied up naked on a cross, jabbed with bamboo poles and taunted for belonging to a foreign superstition.

He was fastened onto bamboo slats that cut into his knees and ice-cold water was poured over him until he went blue. For 14 days the lad endured such brutalities on a near starvation diet. Finally, his body could take no more and he fell into unconsciousness.[26]

The commander of the prison, a samurai named Morioka, felt a sense of shame for having tortured the youth and carried the child to his older sister in the woman's prison. Before he died, Yujiro spoke "words of encouragement," telling his sister that both she and Jinzaburo would survive and return to Nagasaki, and that Jinzaburo's son would become a priest.

A World of Ashes

In June 1934, that Father Moriyama would baptize a young physician, Takashi Nagai, who took as his baptismal name Paul, in honor of the eloquent Jesuit preacher Paul Miki, one of the twenty-six canonized martyrs. Dr. Nagai spoke as an authentic son of Nagasaki when in November 1945 at an open air Requiem Mass in the ruins of Urakami Cathedral he used the word *hansai,* the Japanese word for the biblical holocaust, to describe the atomic bombing: "Was not Nagasaki the chosen victim, the lamb without blemish, slain as a whole burnt offering on an altar of sacrifice, atoning for the sins of all the nations during World War II?"[27]

If there were some among his injured and ill fellow-mourners who were angered by his words, no one could accuse him of being a detached observer. Dr. Nagai was in deep mourning for his beloved wife, Midori, and physically weak from the combined impact of bomb-related injuries and a previously diagnosed underlying leukemia; the leukemia was attributed to radiation exposure in the course of his pioneering diagnostic and research work with X-rays.

Dr. Nagai attributed the bombing, not to blind fate, but to God's purposeful design, and his meditations were shaped by the improbability of it having been dropped on Urakami. The intended target of the bomb, the industrial city of Kokura, was obscured by a cloud cover on August 9, and Major Charles Sweeney flew to Nagasaki, the alternate site, where the bomb was to be dropped over the Mitsubishi Iron Works. Circling to find the target, Major Sweeney realized that he was low on fuel, and when there was a sudden break in the clouds, he gave the order for the bomb to be dropped. Dr. Nagai argued that this remarkable series of random events was proof that it was God's will that Urakami be bombed.

In an instant, eight thousand Christians were called into the hands of God, while in a few hours the fierce flames reduced to ashes this sacred territory of the East. At midnight of that same night the cathedral suddenly burst into flames and was burned to the ground. And exactly at that time in the Imperial Palace, His Majesty the Emperor made known his sacred decision to bring the war to an end.[28]

The people of Nagasaki were left to mourn, to "prostrate themselves before God and pray: Grant that Nagasaki may be the last atomic wilderness in the history of the world."[29]

Dr. Nagai was a patriot whose Shinto family had imbued him with *Nihon-teki,* the expression of the Japanese spirit. He was born in 1908 and raised in Shimane Prefecture, the oldest son (he had four younger siblings) of a physician father, from whom he inherited a love for science. His mother endowed him with respect for intuition and the contemplative spirit; she taught him "how to find the universe in a bowl of rice":

"Look at the rice carefully and discover behind it the countless generations of farmers who pioneered wild land and nurtured rice paddies through droughts and floods, poverty, war and pestilence. See generations of artisans, too, in the simple, practical beauty of the bowl and chopsticks, and all the merchants who handled them. See your parents, too, who worked hard to be able to buy and cook the rice." Nagai's mother would conclude her lesson by joining her hands and bowing in a gesture of profound gratitude.[30]

His childhood years bestowed on him a love of nature, a willingness to accept communal responsibility and familial duty, and a sense of wonder and enjoyment of the world.

At twelve Takashi Nagai was sent to Matsue to attend secondary school, and in 1928 he began his medical studies at the University of Nagasaki. Science and Japanese culture, not faith, were the passions that informed his student years, and he read widely and avidly in the canon of Western thought and literature that came to Japan in the wake of the Meiji Restoration. His mother's death in 1931 initiated a period of profound grief and questioning, beginning a journey to faith that was midwifed by the French mystic scientist Blaise Pascal. Attracted to Catholicism but knowing little about its beliefs and practices, he decided to room with a Catholic family. He was taken in by the Moriyama family, descendants of leaders of the Hidden Christian community; he began to explore Christian beliefs and practices under their example and guidance. More decisively, he fell in love with Midori, the Moriyamas' daughter and only child.

Midori Moriyama and Takashi Nagai were married in 1934 after Nagai returned from a year of military service in Manchuria and after his conversion to Catholicism. His baptism in June 1934 caused a painful split with his father, but in a relatively short time Midori's gentle spirit would repair that rift. Takashi and Midori Nagai had a tender and loving marriage, and she was an unfailing support during the years when he devoted himself to his successful, if meagerly remunerated, research career. An illness on the eve of his medical graduation had left him deaf in one ear; unable to use a stethoscope, he developed a specialty in radiology, which had been newly introduced to Japan in the 1930s. In 1940 he was made an assistant professor and in 1945 became the dean of radiology at the University of Nagasaki.

The Nagais' son, Makoto, was born in 1935, and a daughter, Ikuko, two years later. That same year, Dr. Nagai was conscripted again, mobilized to serve as a surgeon in China with the 5th Division Medical Corps. He was in China when he learned of the deaths of both his father and his infant daughter. He returned to Japan in 1939 as an incipient pacifist. He had seen the brutality of war, but he noted a radical change in attitude from his 1933 service in Manchuria:

> One night he jotted an entry in his notebook about the exhilaration that flooded him that day when he was washing the gangrenous foot of a Chinese soldier-prisoner before an operation. He suddenly realized that he felt the same compassion for a wounded Chinese as for a wounded Japanese, and wrote: "I now know I have come to China not to defeat anybody, not to win a war. I have come to help the wounded, Chinese as much as Japanese, civilians as much as combatants."[31]

He returned to Nagasaki and immersed himself in his pioneering work with X-rays, training physicians in its diagnostic and treatment potential, conducting experiments and writing for medical journals, and, as the war progressed, carrying out increasing responsibilities for civil defense.

In 1941, the same year their daughter Kayano was born, Dr. Nagai was diagnosed with incurable leukemia. He learned of his illness with a sense of guilt over the unnecessary risks he had taken with the X-ray machinery, endangering his health and neglecting his family obligations. Midori's calm faith gave him courage to accept his illness in a spirit of abandonment to God's will.

On August 7, 1945, in response to news of the atomic bombing of Hiroshima, Midori had taken their two children to her mother's nearby rural home; she returned to Nagasaki the next day and was killed instantly by the bomb. Two days later, her grief-stricken husband found her charred remains in her kitchen, a rosary clasped "among the powdered bones of her right hand."[32]

Dr. Nagai was in his office at the medical school, located between three and seven hundred meters from the hypocenter, preparing for a lecture on diagnostic radiology when "the flash of blinding light took place." He thought a bomb had fallen "at the very entrance to the university."

> Broken glass came in like leaves blown off a tree in a whirlwind. I felt that the end had come....It was as though a huge, invisible fist had gone wild and smashed everything in the room....Then the blast of dusty, dirty wind rushed in and filled my nostrils so that I could scarcely breathe.... Everything outside grew dark. There was a noise like the sound of a stormy sea, and the air everywhere swirled round and round.[33]

Co-workers freed him from the rubble and despite his severe cuts and serious loss of blood (his right temporal artery had been cut) Dr. Nagai quickly mobilized the surviving medical personnel into an effective team to rescue the more severely injured patients and staff from the fires that destroyed the hospital in the aftermath of the bomb. For two days, before they were relieved by a military rescue team, they treated victims who laboriously made their way to the once-respected medical facility, only to find it in ruins, its few surviving physicians and nurses frustrated by their lack of medicine and instruments.

> Each life was precious. For all of these people the body was a precious treasure. All were preoccupied with their wounds, big or small. They wanted to be treated by a competent doctor. This was the situation I must somehow face. But then, with this multitude of wounded, with our fast-vanishing medicine, with the flames pressing in, with so few of us...after treating just a few of the wounded I knew that if I did not take a comprehensive view of this situation we would all be engulfed in the flames with the very victims we were bandaging and trying to save.[34]

Dr. Nagai's word portraits of his friends and colleagues elevate *The Bells of Nagasaki* from an account of statistics and factual actions to a moving meditation on the inner life of that small group of twenty medical workers. He writes of the seventeen-year-old student Hashimoto, nicknamed "Little Barrel," who experiences "the ecstatic joy" of being a nurse, a "noble joy accompanied by profound happiness." She and a friend "found a nurse with whom they were vaguely acquainted. Taking her in her arms and carrying her downstairs," she reflects:

> "This Nurse Hamazaki, who's moaning faintly, doesn't know that I'm carrying her out of the flames in my arms.... She'll never know that we saved her life. If we come through all this alive, we'll meet her in the corridor and she'll give a little bow and pass on without any idea of what's happened." And as she reflected on this, a smile vibrated through her cheeks.[35]

Dr. Nagai carried out these rescue obligations despite his growing certainty that Midori had been among the bomb's casualties. Dr. Nagai uses his own story to illustrate the fact that "those who survived the bomb were, if not merely lucky, in a greater or lesser degree selfish, self-centered, guided by instinct and not civilization...and we know it, we who have survived. Knowing it is a dull ache without surcease."[36]

> With the members of my first-aid squad around me, I stayed at the hospital and directed the rescue of the patients. It appeared as if I were perfectly oblivious of myself — I was rendering unselfish service to others, quite as I had always said I would — and afterward I was praised for it by everybody. But inside me, very different feelings were operating. I wanted to run home to my wife. In fact, as I carried one unconscious woman to safety, out of reach of the fire, my thoughts flew to my wife and I became utterly distraught. But I was out to win praise from everybody — I wanted to be called a hero for saving people from the very thick of the blaze without showing my private feelings; *that* was why I kept at it. I was after recognition, so people would say about me, "He did his duty!" Actually, I took no more risks than such recognition would require.[37]

Controversial Spokesman

On August 12, Dr. Nagai and a small group of medical workers left "the world of ashes" that was Nagasaki and made their way to the valley of Mitsuyama, noted for the healing property of its mineral springs. In Koba they established a first aid station and began walking from home to home, village to village, examining and treating the sick with the most basic of medicines. The medical personnel themselves became ill from radiation sickness. Despite hard work, sacrifice, and mourning, Dr. Nagai writes of the tenderness and compassion of those days, when they were fed by farmers who had so generously opened their homes to the survivors, and how they patiently cared for hideously infected wounds and burns. "To show and to receive tender care...this was our life."[38]

In the midst of their labors they fell into despair when they learned that Japan was defeated. "We all held hands and wept. On and on it went. The sun set and the moon rose; but we could not stop weeping.... Our faces, white as milk, sank into a sea of tears. When there were no more tears to shed, the day's fatigue rose to the surface and we fell into a deep sleep."[39] The unending sacrifices of fifteen years of war and the unimaginable wounds of the atomic bomb seemed a futile waste. "Our faith in the eternal stability of the Japanese Empire had crumbled in a moment."[40]

Providing humanitarian aid to the victims of the bomb was Dr. Nagai's strongest motivation, but he was also a passionate scientist whose entire professional career had focused on the atom. It was the supreme irony that Takashi Nagai the scientist could celebrate the victory of science and observe the wounds of the survivors with the avid attentiveness of the inveterate researcher.

> We were members of a research group with a great interest in nuclear physics and totally devoted to this branch of science.... Placed on the experimentation table, we could watch the whole process in a most intimate way.... Crushed with grief because of the defeat of Japan, filled with anger and resentment, we nevertheless felt rising within us a new drive and new motivation in our search for truth. In this devastated atomic desert, fresh and vigorous scientific life began to flourish.[41]

That sense of scientific responsibility led them to make careful observations on the development of radiation disease in their patients and themselves. Dr. Nagai himself collapsed on September 26 and lay close to death; his recovery, on October 5, was considered miraculous. Shortly thereafter, he moved to the ruins of Urakami and built a small, crude shack as a home for his small family: himself, his two children, and his mother-in-law. Eventually, a group of Nagasaki carpenters built him a pilgrim hut next to the shack, and he named it Nyokodo, "love your neighbor as yourself."

It was in that hut that the doctor became a poet, the scientist was transformed into a mystic, and the man who loved the silence and privacy of his research laboratory gave his waning strength to sustain others. His simple hut became a monastic cell in which he contemplated God and the bomb, a man of action who, through sickness and pain, practiced unceasing prayer. It was there that he was given the grace to understand the redemptive nature of suffering, that even such profound losses could be seen and accepted as a part of God's loving Providence. His health failed and he became increasingly debilitated, yet he shared these insights through published writings and letters — with hibakusha, with lepers, with embittered former soldiers, with demoralized citizens of Japan, and with his own children, to prepare them for their impending years as orphans:

> We have forgotten that we are children of God; we have believed in idols; we have disobeyed the law of love. Joyfully we have hated one another; joyfully we have killed one another. And now at last we have brought this great and evil war to an end. But in order to restore peace to the world it was not sufficient to repent. We had to obtain God's pardon through the offering of a great sacrifice.[42]

> Your Christian faith will be no drug that anesthetizes pain. But I can assure you of this: your lonely path is precisely what God in His Providence has chosen specially for you! Accept it as such and often ask Him: How can I use this for Your glory?...Sickness and trouble are not a sign that we are far from God or that He has rejected us....Usefulness is not the point. Our lives are of great worth if we accept with good grace the situation Providence places us in, and go on living lovingly.[43]

Dr. Nagai attained a spirit of profound consolation and peace despite his physical pain and the constraints of time that resulted once he decided to make himself fully available to others. In the six years between the bombing and his death he wrote eleven books. The most famous of those works, *The Bells of Nagasaki,* was completed on August 9, 1946, but Occupation censors refused to permit its publication until January 1949, and then with the proviso that it include a list of Japanese atrocities in the Philippines. (The implicit comparison of the two events may have left Japanese readers with the impression, unintentional on the part of the censor, that both the atomic bomb and Japanese actions in the Philippines deserved to be labeled as atrocities.)

Dr. Nagai was one of the few hibakusha writers allowed to publish during the Occupation, and some have suggested that he was acceptable to authorities precisely because he cast the bomb in a spiritual, not political, framework.

> The question might be, rather, why was Nagai permitted to publish so many books, and why did he agree to the appendix? Answers are not easily forthcoming, for Nagai's relation to the Occupation is still debated. Actually, five of

his books were published in 1949, and three others in the
previous year. Nagai was by far the most published A-bomb
writer during the entire Occupation period. Was he perhaps
the most acceptable to Allied authorities?

My hunch is: yes. Precisely because of his "Nagasaki as
sacrifice" view. Too, his account was too early and factual to
be very political or critical of the winners. He condemns the
war, but not even his own government. And there is no mention of sticky problems like Koreans and other Asians killed
by the bomb, not to mention Allied POWs also annihilated.
The Medical University was in a different part of town.[44]

These are important questions, and it would be interesting to
speculate if, or how, Dr. Nagai's perceptions would have changed
had he lived through the sequel of the 1954 "Lucky Dragon" incident and the subsequent development of a political framework for
hibakusha writing. Dr. Nagai was a spiritual leader, not a political one. He did not gloss over the severity of Nagasaki's "spiritual
wreckage" that "is indeed beyond repair," the "stubborn, unheal-
ing wounds" that the city's survivors carry "deep in our hearts."[45]
It would be incorrect to assume that Dr. Nagai's faith led to passiv-
ity, for his prose was an eloquent protest of the destruction caused
by the bomb.

The fissures which then appeared throughout the blast center
have not yet disappeared, four years later. I am not talking
about cracks in the ground. I am talking about the invisible
chasms which appeared in the personal relationships of the
survivors of that atomic wasteland. These rents in the ties
of friendship and love have not closed up with the passage
of time; on the contrary, they seem to be getting wider and
deeper. They are cracks and fissures in the mutual esteem of
fellow citizens and in their friendship for one another. They
are no more than tiny bits of suspicion and distrust. Yet, of
all the damage the atom bomb did in Nagasaki, they are by
far the cruelest.[46]

He clearly understood the political manipulation of the survivors:

We hear reports of competition in the manufacture of atom
bombs. Yet on reflection it is perfectly clear why such a
dreadful situation should have developed. One reason is that
the destructive power of the atomic bomb is now known to
be less absolute than was at first thought. Hiroshima and Nagasaki were supposed to have been wiped out, but it develops
that, actually, a sizable number of people survived near the

very center of the blasted area.... The people who knead the
strategy of war, therefore, have come around to the notion
that even if the enemy uses an atom bomb, there are ways of
not being defeated by it.

Had the people of Hiroshima and Nagasaki died to a man,
like those of Pompeii, leaving no one to tell the tale, perhaps
even the military strategists would be in awe of the bomb,
and would feel some hesitation at using it. But since, instead, there were survivors, who reported their experience,
the destructive power of the bomb is known to be finite.

And so the physical effects of the bomb are studied, and
found to be bearable. To be surmountable. To be not ir-
reparable.[47] The world had two ugly scars — Hiroshima and
Nagasaki. We thought of these as anti-war vaccinations. But,
when two or three years had passed, it began to appear that
the immunity against war that such vaccinations should have
provided was decreasing.[48]

Despite his progressively worsening health and the need to insure financial support for his children, Dr. Nagai assumed a greater
role as a public figure. The popularity of his books resulted in
a widespread correspondence, and he received numerous visitors,
both the famous (Helen Keller and Emperor Hirohito) and unknown, ordinary citizens. *The Bells of Nagasaki* was made into
a popular movie, and the song of the same title became Nagasaki's unofficial city theme song. In addition to his books, he wrote
countless newspaper and journal articles and gave large sums of
money to help rebuild the institutions of Christian Urakami. None
of this acclaim deflected from his serene acceptance of voluntary
poverty or the constancy of his devotion to God, his children, and
the people of vanquished Japan.

Dr. Nagai received both secular and religious honors: in 1949
he became the first Christian to be honored as a National Hero of
Japan because of his work toward the spiritual restoration of the
country. In May 1949, he received a rosary from Pope Pius XII,
and it was gripped in his hands when he died on May 1, 1951.
Twenty thousand mourners filled the cathedral to mourn his death,
forming a three-mile procession to the graveyard where his ashes
were enshrined. His tombstone bears the simple, eloquent epitaph
from Luke: "We are merely servants: we have done no more than
our duty."

Popular esteem and affection for Dr. Nagai did not mean an un-
critical acceptance of his thinking. One of those who could not
accept Dr. Nagai's spirituality was fellow physician Tatsuichiro
Akizuki. A twenty-nine-year-old Buddhist at the time of the bomb-

ing, Dr. Akizuki was working in a small tuberculosis hospital that had been established in a former Franciscan monastery; he was in the middle of an operation when the bomb fell. *Nagasaki 1945*, Dr. Akizuki's eloquent full-length account of the bombing and his subsequent medical care for survivors, specifically addresses the suffering of innocents. He was blunt with the dying Sister Mizoguchi who "stoically enduring her own pain...spoke words of comfort to me and those near her....The wound in her leg seemed somehow like one of the wounds of Jesus. Why was it, I wondered, that such good and devout people had to be injured and killed?"

> It was hard for me to understand the Catholic or Protestant Christian idea that everything could be attributed to the will and grace of God. It vexed me that these people believed pain and suffering were part of some divine plan. From bitter experience, I couldn't believe in such blind faith, and I mercilessly questioned Sister Mizoguchi and the other innocent, credulous nuns.
>
> "Why is it that *you* have to suffer like this?" I demanded. "Why people like you, who've done nothing but good? It isn't right!"
>
> "I believe in providence," they would reply feebly, but with a smile. "It's the will of God."
>
> I didn't mean to be cruel, questioning such severely burnt people like that. But I had often asked myself such questions....Now the dreadful spectacle of the pain and misery of these pathetic sisters made me doubt yet again the providence of God. But they responded to all my savage questions with a smile, despite their agony.[49]

Referring to Dr. Nagai's tendency "to baptize Nagasaki as an "unblemished lamb," a "suitable sacrifice...acceptable to God," David L. Swain notes that "Akizuki could no more brook this mystification of Nagasaki's hell-on-earth to make it somehow God's will than he could accept the imperial mystification of Japan's warring madness."[50] Dr. Akizuki's writing and publishing efforts have focused on the human suffering caused by the bomb. Recognizing that "we of Nagasaki have failed to communicate our experiences adequately," in 1969 he formed the Society for Nagasaki Testimonies to convey the experience of Nagasaki hibakusha. He is a physician who knows that "terror and suffering always have real names and faces,"[51] and his writing is motivated by "an indelible memory: "The cries of all those people who came to our hospital and died without our being able to treat them properly."[52]

Dr. Akizuki converted to Catholicism in 1949.

Many Nagasaki hibakusha, including Dr. Nagai, had expressed

the hope that the remains of Urakami Cathedral would be preserved as a symbol of Nagasaki's suffering, similar to the A-bomb dome in Hiroshima. Nagasaki city, however, "placing its emphasis on achieving a high level of industrial production and on the tourist industry...has rebuilt with less remembrance than in Hiroshima."[53] Nagasaki is Japan's twenty-fifth largest city, with its current population of 450,000. Its economy remains dominated by Mitsubishi, which, ironically, has shifted to arms production since the decline of Japan's shipbuilding industry.

We live in a time when even Japan is forgetting the "anti-war vaccinations" of Hiroshima and Nagasaki and flirts with military applications of nuclear energy, and so it is not surprising that Dr. Nagai is almost forgotten outside of the Japanese Catholic community. He left no disciples to carry on his work.[54] He is equally unknown in the wider church, which might consider his an arcane spirituality, influenced as it was by his Japanese aesthetic, the legacy of Nagasaki's martyrdom, and a pre–Vatican II spirituality that embraced the Cross as the center of faith. Dr. Nagai was shaped by the unique history of Japanese Catholicism and he, in turn, reflected its luminescent faith to the world.

Takashi Nagai was a responsible citizen of Nagasaki but a busy and private man who was asked to assume a public role: to comfort his neighbors and friends in their hour of need. He responded to their demands with simplicity, modesty, and integrity and lived the final years of his life responding to the grace of this last and temporary vocation. Dr. Nagai knew an unending grief over the loss of his wife and anxiety about the care for his soon to be orphaned children, but he never succumbed to self-pity. He believed that it was a privilege to offer his suffering as part of the fabric of redemption.

"The atomic bomb falling on Nagasaki was a great act of Divine Providence. It was a grace from God. Nagasaki must give thanks to God."[55] Dr. Nagai had a profound reverence for the Cross, and he reflected on the bomb in light of classic Catholic teaching on the redemptive nature of suffering. His focus was on human sinfulness and divine mercy:

Why did we not die with them on that day, at that time, in this house of God? Why must we alone continue this miserable existence?

It is because we are sinners. Ah! Now indeed we are forced to see the enormity of our sins! It is because I have not made expiation for my sins that I am left behind. Those are left who were so deeply rooted in sin that they were not worthy to be offered to God.[56]

When Dr. Nagai was considering conversion he met with Jin-zaburo Moriyama and expressed his distress over the potential rupture of his relationship with his father. Moriyama told Dr. Nagai that, many years after the persecutions, he received a letter from a "Brother Morioka."

> The writer said his father was the official in charge of in-terrogating the Christians at Tsuwano and thus responsible for the death of 36 Christians including Jinzaburo's young brother Yujiro. He, Morioka's son, had become a Christian and joined a religious order. He enclosed money to cover travel expenses in the hope that Jinzaburo would do him the great favor of meeting him in Tsuwano. Jinzaburo went, met him at Tsuwano railway station and the two walked 20 min-utes in silence to the site of the prison camp, just beyond the town....
>
> Jinzaburo sank to his knees. In a flash Br. Morioka was kneeling beside him, his forehead almost to the ground, sob-bing out his sorrow for what his father had done to them. Jinzaburo turned and embraced him. "Your father thought he was doing his duty as a government official. He really believed the Christian faith was subversive and a danger to Japan.... You know, I have prayed for your father ever since and I am sure Yujiro prays for him from heaven. Knowing that you have been given the Faith makes my brother's death all the more meaningful. It is another example of the great truth that you understand better than me, Brother — God is always in charge; difficulties, darkness and suffering become opportunities for new graces if we keep trusting."[57]

Takashi Nagai was faithful to the same spirit that sustained his patron, St. Paul Miki. He witnessed to the radiant optimism of a radical humility that sees all things as being from the loving hand of God. He never wavered from the faith that allowed him to see "the depths of God's friendship" in Urakami's nuclear wasteland.

6

In the Company of Hibakusha

——— ⅋ ———

There are several conventional ways of perceiving Hiroshima, each of which yields certain metaphors. One view, held by those who claim to be realists, argues that it was necessary to use the bomb to end the war, that it saved tens of thousands of Japanese and American lives that would have been lost had there been an Allied invasion of the Japanese mainland. People who hold this belief stress the physical power of the bomb but generally omit reference to the delayed effects of radiation. They justify the use of the bomb by calling forth the names of Japanese atrocities. In this metaphor Hiroshima is a symbol of the just use of power, the hard morality of war, and to think otherwise is to be foolishly naive and sentimental.

> Nothing is more natural for a democracy at war than for its leader — elected by the people and answerable to them — to attempt to ensure that victory is attained with the minimum loss of soldiers' lives. For an industrial democracy, firepower is the means to that end. The almost extravagant use of material firepower in order to save young men's lives has been called, rightly, "the American way of war." Using the atom bomb against Japan was simply the ultimate step in an approach to war that marked the Pacific conflict from the moment Douglas MacArthur took command.[1]

Another attitude, shared by those in the peace movement, contends that the atom bombs were totally unjustifiable atrocities that ushered in the nuclear age. In this metaphor, Hiroshima and Nagasaki are code words for nuclear destruction, and hibakusha are the living symbols of what might happen to all of us if those weapons are used again. They argue that everything must be done not only to prevent their future use but to work for the abolition of nuclear weapons. There is an inherent idealism in this attitude, but there is enough cynicism for peace groups to explicitly request that only visibly scarred hibakusha speak at rallies. Dr. Tadatoshi

Akiba once expressed the opinion that self-protection, rather than any anti-nuclear philosophy, was the motivation of the mainstream American peace groups in the 1980s.

His observation, if it is accurate, suggests that there is a widespread perception that hibakusha should be "studied" for the benefit of all people. Hibakusha justly resent being treated as guinea pigs by researchers who rather blithely claimed that, whether or not the use of the bomb was justified, it *was* dropped, and it would be irresponsible not to study hibakusha to learn about the delayed effects of radiation exposure. (How wasteful not to take advantage of this living laboratory!)

Each August, adherents of these two views talk at each other through newspaper columns and letters.

> The real meaning of Hiroshima is that war is an extremely nasty business, and that we must do everything consonant with our freedom and our honor to assure that such terrible events do not recur. Modern warfare is particularly trying on the conscience of decent people because the tension between the need to save one's own men and the requirement indiscriminately to kill the enemy's rises with each "improvement" in the destructive capacity of the weapons.[2]

> It was a very nice gesture indeed to toll the bells across the nation for Hiroshima. However, I do not recall the same thing taking place on Dec. 7.
>
> Let us not forget that the Japanese people [at Hiroshima] are no more dead than our men at Pearl Harbor. Also, the atomic bombing of Hiroshima was not a sneak attack.[3]

> Those people who died at Hiroshima and later at Nagasaki were killed by the atomic bomb, but they really died because of an evil Japanese ideology. There was scarcely a crime the Japanese had not committed in their drive to conquer the world. Today's Japanese are uncompromising in their commitment to peace. They're forever coming up and thanking Americans for setting Japan on the road to democracy. So for the Japanese, Hiroshima was a terrible lesson, but they appear to have learned it well.[4]

> I don't believe it is possible for one who did not live through the war years to fully appreciate the loathing with which the Japanese were regarded. The sneak attack on Pearl Harbor started it.[5]

> We gave the Japanese less than 72 hours to understand a weapon of mind-boggling destruction that had never before

existed; to comprehend an experience that could not have even been imagined; and to process a horror that had never before been experienced in the history of humankind.... Could I explain how I felt anything but pride that my country was the first and only nation to use atomic weapons against other human beings?[6]

We have lost the ability to relate to Hiroshima; these arguments about the bomb are code words for a host of political, religious, and social attitudes. They either ignore hibakusha or relegate them to such rarefied symbolic roles that they lose all of their individuality and uniqueness. We have all been affected by the atomic bomb but only hibakusha experienced it, and so it is all the more ironic that we have denied them their central teaching role. Hibakusha have been ill-treated, whether in Japan (despite limited financial and medical security) or the United States or Korea. The social and economic discrimination they have faced is only a visible expression of a deeper societal contempt, part of which is due to the traditional treatment of the handicapped. During my stay at the World Friendship Center the resident translator/secretary was a young woman who suffered from a congenital deformity, a harelip that resulted in a speech impediment, and I suspect that part of her fierce identification with hibakusha, although she was not native to Hiroshima, was due to the cruelty she had experienced from schoolmates in her rural community. She was justly angry about and quite eloquent in detailing the treatment of the handicapped in Japan, and she helped me understand the depth of contempt experienced by many disabled people.

A percentage of hibakusha are scarred from burns and some are disabled from bomb-related injuries, but radiation's most decisive injury is invisible, the way it disrupts and alters the genetic structure of cells. In recent years there have been parallels made between the historical treatment of lepers (notably the association of contagion and sin) and the response to people with AIDS, which adds a burden of isolation and discrimination to the ravages of the disease. The same pattern can be seen in our response to hibakusha, who, because they bear the invisible deformity of radiation, are contemporary symbols of powerlessness. It is the tenor of our fear that condemns hibakusha to their haunting isolation. The very existence of hibakusha reminds us how fragile our security is, how tentative our safety. It is very human to run from powerlessness but history has shown that structures created for safety inevitably become even more dangerous idols.

The metaphor of idolatry has allowed me an unrestricted, expansive view of Hiroshima as compared with the constriction of political metaphors. In this view, hibakusha are not only the first victims and first survivors, but also the first prophets of the nuclear age. It is a calling they have assumed with modesty and a sense of proportion. It has always impressed me that hibakusha, inculcated as they were in the mythology of imperial Japan, could realize the futility of nationalism and become genuine citizens of the world. They understand that all peoples of the world now share a common threat, and hibakusha have acted to foster that awareness with the slim hope that realization of the threat will lead to acts of self-preservation through disarmament and mutual cooperation.

For many years I associated Hiroshima with an intense silence. The first time I experienced that quality was when, as a young teenager, I met a survivor of the Holocaust. She was an older, quite ordinary looking woman who sat down next to me on a bus, and when she took off her coat and reached up to stow it on the overhead rack I saw the blue numbers tattooed on the wrinkled, sagging flesh of her inner arm. The tenor of that two-hour trip remains vivid for me, a mingling of shyness, curiosity about her experiences (a curiosity that seemed somewhat shameful to me) and, although I did not know what name to give it, a desire to pay homage to the sheer fact of this woman's survival.

I had the same response the first few times I heard hibakusha speak and remembered it again when I read Edita Morris's evocative novel *The Flowers of Hiroshima*. That book ends with the death of Fumio, the narrator's husband, from a radiation-related illness:

> He tries to smile, but a spasm of pain twists his face. His whole body contracts. My husband lies there fighting with pain as a man might wrestle with a lion....I can hear them panting in that terrible life-or-death embrace.
>
> It's Fumio who wins! I know it when he smiles, and impulsively I begin to bow. Kneeling on the floor, I bow and bow to the victor — to the victim and the sufferer — to the great human being who is my husband. As he sees me paying homage to his suffering and his triumph, tears form in my husband's eyes, glisten for a second on his long lashes, then like minute rivers course through that landscape of agony which once was a human face. The tears skirt the ridges of his dried blisters, run over the live sores, make their way into his open mouth.[7]

I was all the more surprised and troubled that when I finally went to Hiroshima my emotional response to hibakusha was blunted and at times even skirted the edges of cynicism. Psychologists have noted that psychic numbing is a common defense that hampers people from dealing with nuclear issues, and I knew that my emotional detachment was a way to protect myself from the horror evoked by stories of the bomb, even those told at a distance of almost forty years. There were other times when I was so absorbed in someone's story that I experienced a momentary disorientation to find myself in the vital, functioning city of modern-day Hiroshima. I met people with whom I wept and others whose moral courage inspired in me such a fierce respect that I wanted to "bow to the victim and the sufferer."

I returned to the United States and began writing about hibakusha. I had become more conservative in the years after leaving the Community for Creative Nonviolence, and with age and changed life circumstances I was less inclined to activism — not that I had ever looked forward to participating in acts of civil disobedience; more often my motivation was the need to save face among my peers rather than a deep commitment to social justice. Still I did feel the desire to do some work for peace, and writing about Hiroshima and Nagasaki seemed to be a modest and responsible contribution to the larger anti-nuclear community. I continued with my research and writing, participated in educational programs about Hiroshima, and, in order to develop greater sensitivity to hibakusha, I studied Japanese for three years, certain, at times, that it would have been easier to go to jail.

Barbara Reynolds often quoted an elderly hibakusha who had told her that American peace activists, with the luxury of their transient enthusiasms, were like pine branches, "quick to flare up and just as quick to die down." I think that on some level Barbara was determined to prove him wrong, as if her long and steadfast involvement with Hiroshima would ameliorate this man's judgment on all Americans.

As for myself, I took no small amount of pride in the relative longevity of my commitment, but there came a time when that man's words would haunt me. In 1991 I began to notice actions that belied a lack of enthusiasm about Hiroshima. Books I had once bought and read with avid and genuine interest became obligatory purchases that remained on my shelves, unopened for months. Letters from peers and teachers in Japan and the United States went unanswered, and it was rare for me to initiate a correspondence, even with someone I admired. It took work to develop the emotional energy to visit hibakusha when they came to Boston on speaking tours and at times it seemed as if boredom was my response to the very name of Hiroshima.

I read a lot about Japanese culture before going to Hiroshima, and although I cannot remember where I read it, I recall a vivid simile that likened Japan to an onion. Based on his own experiences, the author made a convincing argument that as soon as you think you can describe Japan, a layer peels away, and you are left with a reality you know nothing about. That image was apt as I set out to understand what compelled my involvement with Hiroshima. It was symptomatic of my underlying malaise that self-absorbed questions replaced more disciplined study and writing. Was it only pride that kept me from giving up work that had been such an important part of my identity for seven years? Why had I attained so little in the way of career or academic advancement for all those hours of work? The layers that peeled away were only negative answers: I knew it was not a scholarly labor, because I am not an intellectual and I had no interest in pursuing a career as a journalist. I also knew that, despite a genuine opposition to nuclear weapons, I did not have the vocation to be a peacemaker.

I gained some clues to my motivation from Barbara Reynolds. From its earliest days our friendship took on the contours of a mentor-student relationship, and I consciously thought of Barbara as a role model and teacher. For two women of such different ages and life experiences we shared similar styles of negotiating the world; both of us were intuitive and enjoyed long, introspective conversations. I learned a lot from our talks because Barbara was remarkably open in discussing the formative experiences of her time in Hiroshima.

It was through these conversations that I began to see how patterns of emotional need give shape to social commitments. Barbara had a deep empathy for and identification with hibakusha; in actual fact she was one, having been exposed to radioactive fallout during the *Phoenix* protest, but her passion about Hiroshima was fueled by more intimate coincidences.

Abandonment was one of the major themes of Barbara's autobiographical narrative. Her experience of loss began with her father's untimely death when she was fifteen and intensified with her devastating mid-life divorce from Earle Reynolds. The divorce and her almost reckless generosity in funding the Peace Study Mission left her financially insecure and literally and emotionally homeless. Barbara transformed that material deprivation into a positive embrace of voluntary poverty, sustained by the faith that became increasingly central in her life. For many years after her return to the United States she was a veritable pilgrim, living with family or friends or in institutional settings; when she finally settled in a small apartment in Long Beach, California (several miles from her daughter), she opened her home to Vietnamese and Cambodian refugees.

Her religious commitments provided Barbara with genuine spiritual and emotional succor. She interpreted everything that hap-

pened to her through the prism of her faith, saw all of her
experiences as a revelation of God's will for herself. Barbara had
a ready gratitude for the good things in her life, but it was common for her to interpret difficulties as God's chastisement for her
"disobedience." The rapidity with which she reached that conclusion suggested to me that she very much wanted to avoid anger
and feared its consequences, particularly when it was directed to
authority figures. Similarly, she circumvented sadness by reminding
herself that her suffering was minimal compared to that of hibakusha who had, she often said, "lost everything." She looked at her
losses as opportunities to grow in empathy for hibakusha.

In the months before Barbara's death I began to notice a sense
of irritation at the conclusion of our telephone conversations, and
I interpreted these feelings as frustration with the mentor-student
roles we had long played for each other. I am sure that part of what
I mourned, in the weeks after Barbara's unexpected death, was the
lost opportunity for a genuine friendship. But even as I acknowledged that frustration I never lost my admiration for Barbara's life
of service, a life that I came to see as a parable of redemptive
suffering. The tears that Barbara could not shed for herself were
given to mourn others; her loneliness led her to embrace those
more lonely and marginal and to form a community of compassion that transcended race and ethnicity; the anger that she could
not marshall on her own behalf was transformed into a passion
for justice.

Once I saw these patterns in Barbara's life I was able to understand that I was drawn to hibakusha not only for altruistic reasons,
but because of a deep identification with their experience. It is not
uncommon for the choice of career or an area of social involvement to reflect, and in some ways resolve, emotional needs. I am
certain that my years of work with the homeless in Washington,
D.C., was an outward expression of what I now recognize was a
sense of emotional homelessness, so that in caring for others I was
trying to ameliorate my own unhappiness. I saw a more vibrant expression of this in hibakusha, whose terrible losses were not healed,
but somehow attenuated by their work for peace.

As important as my work with the homeless was, I had known
no previous commitment to a cause that was as passionate or inexplicable as my involvement with hibakusha. Despite having briefly
considered applying to work at the World Friendship Center, I
knew that the language barrier would limit whatever care I could
give to individual hibakusha. On the train from Tokyo to Hiroshima I fantasized about volunteering at the A-bomb Hospital, of
learning about the bomb by bathing and feeding and attending to
the daily needs of ill and infirm hibakusha, a hidden, silent novi-

tiate rather than the public month of many words. I often think it would have been a wiser choice.

I felt a kinship with hibakusha, I, who had always known myself to be an outsider, and hibakusha, true outsiders because their A-bomb experience has indelibly marked them unique. Like Barbara, I hated anger and in adopting hibakusha as my role models I sought a way to emulate the "good victim" — "it is war we hate, not Americans" — who had (seemingly) transcended anger through a public stance of self-sacrifice and service. I was attracted to the astringent heroism of hibakusha and admired their refusal to engage in self-pity, which for a long time had been my temptation and trap, and their embrace of a particularly generous altruism.

I read my own story in the pages of Hiroshima's, and because it was safe, I was able, intellectually, to explore the themes that I would eventually gain the courage to confront emotionally. It was through the stories of hibakusha that I learned about the demands of loyalty, the nature of reconciliation, and how to accept and understand loss. I like to think that the actual and metaphoric years I spent in the company of hibakusha allowed me to absorb enough of their courage, dignity, and resilience so that eventually I was able to close the text of Hiroshima and read and resolve my own grief and anger. It was a long journey, from the purity of heart with which I first listened to hibakusha to the convoluted emotions of politics and psychology, but at the end of the journey I was graced with these stories of healing, transformation, generosity, and reconciliation. It is my privilege to pass them on so that others might find their place in the city of silence and hope.

Notes

─── ❧ ───

Introduction

1. *Nuclear Fear: A History of Images* by Spencer Weart (Cambridge, Mass.: Harvard University Press, 1988) offers a lucid examination of the psychological ramifications of the key images of the nuclear age and the manner in which public opinion was manipulated for political reasons. Weart, who is both a physicist and a historian, offers a skillful interpretation of popular, historical, and scholarly material. He develops a complex but compelling vision of the nuclear age that is sober and challenging, but not without hope.

2. The photographer Robert Del Tredici has documented the nuclear industry in the striking book *At Work in the Fields of the Bomb* (New York: Harper & Row, 1987). While working on a previous book (*The People of Three Mile Island* [San Francisco: Sierra Club Books, 1980]) Del Tredici was startled to realize that he had never seen a nuclear weapon, and that simple observation sent him on a journey to make visible the world of nuclear weapons plants. In addition to photographs of the plants, Del Tredici includes portraits and transcripts of interviews with scientists, atomic veterans, hibakusha, and "downwinders." He deals with the environmental degradation that resulted from Chernobyl, atmospheric nuclear tests in the Pacific, and power plants in the United States.

3. Robert Lifton's psychological profile of hibakusha, *Death in Life: Survivors of Hiroshima* (New York: Random House, 1967), remains one of the more influential books about Hiroshima, although critics (primarily Japanese, but also some Americans) have questioned his emphasis on hibakusha's "death imprint" and their subsequent survivor guilt. Lifton's work is most helpful in its portrayal of hibakusha activists and the description of some of the problems faced by artists and commentators as they try to convey their experience of the bomb.

The most important resource for any serious student of the bombings is the Hiroshima/Nagasaki Memorial Collection, part of the Peace Resource Center at Wilmington College. The Center has an excellent lending library of books, audio and video tapes, curricula, and archival material on the bomb, peace studies, and conflict resolution. The Center, which for many years has been under the able direction of Helen Redding Wiegel, publishes a quarterly newsletter with excellent annotated bibliographies. For more information, contact: Hiroshima/Nagasaki Memorial Collection, Peace Resource Center, Wilmington College, Wilmington, OH 45177.

Chapter 1 – City of Silence and Hope: Hiroshima

1. Information specific to Nagasaki is addressed in chapter 5. Although in the present chapter I make reference to Hiroshima alone, general information about the effects of the bomb applies to hibakusha from both cities.

2. Setsuko Thurlow, "The Atomic Bombing of Hiroshima and Nagasaki: The Role of Women in the Japanese Peace Movement," in *Women and Peace,* ed. Ruth Roach Pierson (London: Croom Helm, 1987), 226.

3. Kenzaburo Oe, *Hiroshima Notes,* ed. David L. Swain, trans. Toshi Yonezawa (Tokyo: YMCA Press, 1981), 171.

4. There were nine "double hibakusha" who experienced both bombs; all were residents of Nagasaki who were in Hiroshima on August 6, and returned to their homes by August 9. Their remarkable stories are told in Robert Trumbull's book, *Nine Who Survived Hiroshima and Nagasaki* (New York: Dutton, 1957).

5. Discussion of the political and diplomatic circumstances of the decision to use the bomb is outside the scope of this study. The following are recommended for a fuller treatment of this debate. There is an excellent bibliographic essay included in Martin J. Sherwin's, *A World Destroyed: The Atomic Bomb and the Grand Alliance* (New York: Knopf, 1975). Gar Alperovitz's classic, *Atomic Diplomacy* (New York: Simon and Schuster, 1965, 1985), has a new introduction in its revised edition. A serious student of the bomb would do well to read Richard Rhodes, *The Making of the Atomic Bomb* (New York: Simon and Schuster, 1986).

6. *The Effects of Atomic Bombs on Hiroshima and Nagasaki,* U.S. Strategic Bombing Survey Reports, Pacific War: no. 3 (Washington, D.C.: Government Printing Office, 1946), 22.

7. Historian John Dower explores the role of race in the Pacific War by analyzing both Japanese and American propaganda in *War without Mercy: Race and Power in the Pacific War* (New York: Pantheon Books, 1986). The bomb was developed in response to fears by refugee scientists that German nuclear physics was more advanced than Allied knowledge; the war in Europe was over before work on the atomic bomb was completed. Information on the Japanese effort to develop an atomic bomb is included in *The Day Man Lost: Hiroshima, 6 August 1945* by the Pacific War Research Society (New York: Kodansha, 1981). The book is critical of the militarists who delayed the decision to end the war.

8. Robert Karl Manoff, "The Media: Nuclear Secrecy vs. Democracy," *Bulletin of Atomic Scientists* 40 (January 1984): 73.

9. Burchett revisited Hiroshima in 1971 and subsequently wrote *Shadows of Hiroshima* (London: Verso, 1983).

10. Naomi Shohno, *The Legacy of Hiroshima: Its Past, Our Future,* trans. Tomoko Nakamura, adapt. Jeffrey Hunter (Tokyo: Kosei, 1986), 15.

11. The Committee for the Compilation of Materials on Damage Caused by the Atomic Bombs in Hiroshima and Nagasaki, *The Impact of the A-Bomb: Hiroshima and Nagasaki, 1945–85,* trans. Eisei Ishikawa and David L. Swain (Tokyo: Iwanami Shoten, 1985), 28–29.

12. Ibid., 31.

13. The narrative of Masuji Ibuse's *Black Rain,* trans. John Bester (New York: Kodansha, 1979) — arguably the most famous Hiroshima novel — concerns a man's effort to find a marriage partner for his young niece who, although not in Hiroshima on the day of the bombing, had received significant radiation exposure from black rain.

14. Setsuko Thurlow, "Silent Flash of Light," *Saturday Night* 100 (August 1985): 32.

15. Committee, *Impact of the A-Bomb,* 31–32.

16. "Excerpts from *Recollections and Reflections of Pedro Arrupe, S.J.,*" *America* 16 (February 1991): 184–85. Father Arrupe (1907–91) was the superior general of the Jesuits from 1965 to 1983. In August 1945, he was in residence at the Jesuit novitiate in Nagatsuka, six kilometers from the hypocenter; although he was thrown to the floor by the blast effect he was spared serious injury. The Jesuits set up a first aid station in their damaged but intact building and were able to accommodate and treat 150 survivors; remarkably, only one of them died.

17. Committee, *Impact of the A-Bomb,* 104–5.

18. *The Effects of Atomic Bombs on Hiroshima and Nagasaki,* 19.

19. Ichiro Moritaki, "New Morality for the Atomic Age" (Hiroshima: Hiroshima University, photocopy), 1.

20. Shohno, *Legacy of Hiroshima,* 131

21. "Code for Japanese Press," General Headquarters, United States Army Forces, Pacific, September 21, 1945.

22. Keiko Doi, interview by author, Hiroshima, Japan, May 12, 1984.

23. ABCC conducted studies on the 283,000 survivors identified in the 1950 Japanese census. Their physical and laboratory findings are matched with non-hibakusha controls.

24. Thurlow, "Women in the Peace Movement," 228–29.

25. Paul Boyer, *By the Bomb's Early Light: American Thought and Culture at the Dawn of the Atomic Age* (New York: Pantheon, 1985), 210.

26. Robert Lifton, *Death in Life: Survivors of Hiroshima* (New York: Random House, 1967), 213.

27. Yoshiteru Kosakai, *Hiroshima Peace Reader,* trans. Akira and Michiko Tashiro and Robert and Alice Ruth Ramseyer (Hiroshima: Hiroshima Peace Culture Foundation, 1983), 46.

28. Ibid., 47.

29. *The Impact of the A-Bomb,* 183.

30. Norma Field, *In the Realm of the Dying Emperor* (New York: Pantheon, 1991), 259–60.

31. Ibid., 178.

32. Ibid., 254.

33. Steven R. Weisman, "At Atomic Shrine, All the Horror, Nothing of Guilt," *New York Times,* April 19, 1990.

34. David L. Swain, letter to author, October 30, 1994.

35. Moritaki, "New Morality," 1.

36. Ibid., 8.

37. Lifton, *Death in Life,* 228.

38. Susumu Ishitani, "On *Hadashi no Gen*," in Kathryn Taylor Mizuno and Susumu Ishitani, eds., *Social Concerns in Japan*, (Tokyo: Apollonsha, 1980), 64–65. This essay also appears as the introduction to the English translation of *Hadashi no Gen* (*Barefoot Gen*), which originally appeared as serialized cartoons in Japan in 1972–73. *Barefoot Gen: A Cartoon Story of Hiroshima* (Philadelphia: New Society Publishers, 1987) and *Barefoot Gen: The Day After* (Philadelphia: New Society Publishers, 1988) are based on the Hiroshima experience of cartoonist Keiji Nakazawa. Its autobiographical narrator, a young boy, tells of the persecution his family endured because of his father's staunch anti-militarism. The books portray a Japan exhausted by fifteen years of war, the physical and social effects of the bombing, and the attempts of hibakusha to obtain food, shelter, and medical care. Nakazawa raises important ethical issues about discriminatory treatment of Koreans, the social pressures of conformity, and the courage of individuals who withstood such pressure.

Chapter 2 – "I Met the Bomb at . . ."

1. The Committee for the Compilation of Materials on Damage Caused by the Atomic Bombs in Hiroshima and Nagasaki, *Hiroshima and Nagasaki: The Physical, Medical and Social Effects of the Atomic Bombings,* trans. Eisei Ishikawa and David L. Swain (New York: Basic Books, 1981), 586.

2. Agawa, who was born in Hiroshima, was not exposed to the bomb, although his parents were. He returned to Hiroshima in March 1946. The narrative of *Devil's Heritage* (trans. John Maki [Tokyo: Hokuseido, 1957]) is told through a Tokyo reporter and fictionalizes hibakusha attitudes toward ABCC. Ibuse's *Black Rain* uses the diary format to explore social discrimination against hibakusha. Ibuse's is the title story in *The Crazy Iris and Other Stories of the Atomic Aftermath* (ed. Kenzaburo Oe [New York: Grove, 1985]). Of the nine authors represented in this collection only one is a hibakusha who is not a professional writer; all the others are hibakusha who were established writers before August 1945 or non-hibakusha professional writers. Hiroshima-born Yoko Ota (1906–63) was already an important novelist when she experienced the bomb in 1945. Censors required her to rework *Town of Corpses* (completed in 1946), and it was published in 1948.

Robert Lifton offers an insightful analysis of atomic bomb literature and the dilemmas of the artist in *Death in Life: Survivors of Hiroshima* (New York: Random House, 1967). "Artistic re-creation of an overwhelming historical experience has much to do with the question of mastery. Artists can apply to that experience their particular aesthetic traditions and individual talents to evolve new ways of 'seeing' it and giving it form" (*Death in Life,* 397).

Kyoko and Mark Selden have compiled the excellent *The Atomic Bomb: Voices from Hiroshima and Nagasaki* (Armonk, N.Y.: M. E. Sharpe, 1989) with entries that include fiction, personal narratives, and poetry, many of which had not previously been translated. The excellent introductory essay, which provides a historical overview of the deci-sion to use the bomb, and the deft choice of selections, which point to little-known dimensions of the atomic bomb experience, make this a thoughtful, valuable addition to the literature on the atomic bomb.

3. One of the earliest physician memoirs to be translated into English (and therefore influential in shaping an American understanding of the human cost of the bomb) was Michihiko Hachiya's *Hiroshima Diary: The Journal of a Japanese Physician, August 6–September 30, 1945*, trans. and ed. Warner Wells (Chapel Hill: University of North Carolina Press, 1955). Dr. Hachiya was the director of the Hiroshima Communications Hospital (1.4 kilometers from the hypocenter), one of four major civilian hospitals in the city.

4. Arata Osada, "Compiler's Letter to the Writers," in *Children of the A-Bomb: The Testament of the Boys and Girls of Hiroshima,* comp. Dr. Arata Osada, trans. Jean Dan and Ruth Sieben-Morgen (New York: Putnam's, 1963), 253.

5. For information on the availability of these and other films contact the Hiroshima/Nagasaki Memorial Collection, Peace Resource Center, Wilmington College, Wilmington, OH 45177.

6. Hirotu Kubouro, interview by author, Hiroshima, Japan, May 14, 1984.

7. Osada, *Children of the A-Bomb,* 254.

8. Sadako Ueno, "Survival under the A-Bomb Cloud," in *Survival under Atomic Bomb* (Hiroshima, privately published, n.d.), 65–66.

9. Transcript of English translation of hibakusha testimony. In the aftermath of the bomb, many people complained of a horrible thirst and a feeling of burning, of having swallowed a toxic substance, but there was a rumor that giving water to the victims would be inevitably fatal. In an effort to assuage their terrible thirst, many people tried to drink from the river, from water tanks, or from cisterns. The feeble cries of hundreds of victims begging for water is one of the most compelling images that hibakusha narrate.

10. Hiroshi Sawachika, "The Experience of an Army Surgeon in Treating Atomic Bomb Survivors on 6 August 1945," in Teruaki Fuku-hara, M.D., *Hiroshima in the Summer of 1945* (Hiroshima: privately published, no date), 11–12.

11. Japanese Broadcasting Corporation (NHK), ed., *Unforgettable Fire: Pictures Drawn by Atomic Bomb Survivors,* trans. World Friendship Center, Hiroshima (New York: Pantheon, 1977), 46.

12. Ibid., 48.

13. Ibid., 51.

14. Ibid., 96.

15. Yoshiko Motoyasu, "The Wounds of Hate," in *Survival under Atomic Bomb,* 68–69.

16. Tameko Fukuda, "Hiroshima in September," in Committee for Peace and Nuclear Disarmament, *Testimonies of Hiroshima and Naga-saki: Lutheran Hibakusha and Their Families* (Hiroshima: Japan Evangel-ical Lutheran Church, 1984), 47.

17. *Children of the A-Bomb,* 50–51.

18. Itsuo Kojima, "Excessive Cruelty," in *Survival under Atomic Bomb,* 70.

19. Hitoshi Takayama, "Atomic Bomb Experience and the Suffering of Victims," in *Testimonies of Hiroshima and Nagasaki,* 34.

20. Tatsuichiro Akizuki, *Nagasaki 1945,* trans. Keiichi Nagata (London: Quartet Books, 1981), 101, 103.

21. Tokihiko Shimizu, "My Experience of the Atomic Bomb in Nagasaki," in *Testimonies of Hiroshima and Nagasaki,* 53.

22. Transcript of English translation of hibakusha testimony.

23. Kayako Nakanishi, "My Hiroshima Atomic Bomb Experience," in *Testimonies of Hiroshima and Nagasaki,* 9.

24. *Children of the A-Bomb,* 84.

25. Transcript of English translation of hibakusha testimony.

26. Transcript of English translation of hibakusha testimony.

27. *Children of the A-Bomb,* 128.

28. Transcript of English translation of hibakusha testimony.

29. Transcript of English translation of hibakusha testimony.

30. Fumi Itoh, "That Child Is Not Dead!" in "A Voice from Heaven: Personal Memories of the Hiroshima Holocaust," comp. of the Japanese editions (1949 and 1983) Toshio Suekane; trans. Ian G. MacLeod; ed. of English edition David L. Swain, unpublished, typescript, 1985, 40–44.

31. Hisae Aoki, "Back from Death's Doorstep," in *Testimonies of the Atomic Bomb Survivors: A Record of the Devastation of Nagasaki,* trans. Brian Burke-Gaffney (Nagasaki: City of Nagasaki, 1985), 88.

32. Transcript of English translation of hibakusha testimony.

33. Tsukasa Uchida, "Thirty Five Years after the Atomic Bombing," in *Testimonies of the Atomic Bomb Survivors,* 139–40.

34. Transcript of English translation of hibakusha testimony.

35. Transcript of English translation of hibakusha testimony.

36. Transcript of English translation of hibakusha testimony.

37. Hisashi Aoki, "The Unforgettable Hell," in *Testimonies of the Atomic Bomb Survivors,* 98.

38. Sadako Kurihara, "We Shall Bring Forth New Life," trans. Wayne Lammers, in Sadako Kurihara, ed., *The Songs of Hiroshima* (Hiroshima: Anthology Publishing Association, 1980), 21.

39. Sadako Kurihara, "The Suffering of Writers Who Experienced Hiroshima, and Contemporary Literature on the Subject of the Atomic Bomb" (lecture text), in Kurihara, *The Songs of Hiroshima,* 22–23.

40. Akizuki, *Nagasaki 1945,* 144–45.

Chapter 3 – The Symbolic American: Barbara Reynolds

1. Sam Totten and Martha Wescoat Totten, *Facing the Danger: Interviews with 20 Anti-Nuclear Activists* (Trumansburg, N.Y.: Crossing Press, 1984), 72.

2. I corresponded with Barbara from December 1984 until her death in February 1990. In August 1988 I spent three days at her home in Long Beach, California, and the following April we spent a week together at

Wilmington College (in Wilmington, Ohio) and examined some of her letters and papers archived in the Hiroshima-Nagasaki Memorial Collection. In writing this chapter I have drawn from her published writings, the letters she wrote me, and six hours of conversation taped during that 1989 visit.

Hiroshima extended honorary citizenship to Norman Cousins in 1964 in recognition of the Moral Adoption Movement and Hiroshima Maidens project. Ira and Edita Morris were honored in 1967 for their writing and the founding of Hiroshima House, which provided recreation and hospitality for hibakusha. In 1968 Father Hugo Lassale, a naturalized Japanese citizen of German descent, was recognized for his efforts to construct the World Peace Memorial Cathedral. In 1980 the Methodist missionary Mary McMillan received both honorary citizenship in Hiroshima and the Imperial Fourth Order of the Sacred Treasure. Floyd Schmoe was honored in 1983.

3. The story of the Hiroshima Maidens project is told in Rodney Barker's *Hiroshima Maidens* (New York: Viking, 1985). Barker was a child when his Connecticut family hosted two of the Maidens. His book details the social dislocation these women faced when they returned to Japan, including the necessity of coping with jealousy from the many hibakusha who were denied opportunities for rehabilitation. The fortieth anniversary edition of *Hiroshima* (New York: Knopf, 1985) also includes information on the project, but Barker and Hersey offer different interpretations of the eventual strains in the relationship between Cousins and Tanimoto, perhaps inevitable difficulties (despite a reservoir of good will) in such an ambitious bicultural program that was laden with symbolic and emotional freight.

In his autobiography, *Hiroshima Surgeon,* Tomin Harada, M.D. (trans. Robert L. and Alice R. Ramseyer [Newton, Kans.: Faith and Life Press, 1983]) has an interesting chapter about his pioneering work with reconstructive surgery for hibakusha and his eventual participation in the Hiroshima Maidens project. In 1967, Dr. Harada arranged for napalm-injured women from Vietnam to travel to Hiroshima to receive plastic surgery. Dr. Harada was a close friend and colleague of Barbara Reynolds and for many years he served as chairman of the board of the Friendship Center.

4. Edita Morris is the author of *The Flowers of Hiroshima* (New York: Pocket Books, 1963), which was awarded the Albert Schweitzer Literary Prize, and *The Seeds of Hiroshima* (New York: Braziller, 1966). In deceptively simple, elegant prose, Morris narrates the story of a young American businessman and the hibakusha family with whom he boards; gradually he, and the reader, come to understand the suffering hidden behind the facade of a city being restored to economic health. Unfortunately both of these lovely, deeply felt novels are out of print.

5. Robert Lifton offers a lucid delineation of the complex relationships between hibakusha and Americans in the chapter "Perceiving America" in *Death in Life: Survivors of Hiroshima* (New York: Random House, 1967). Lifton's concept of counterfeit nurturance is particularly germane to a discussion of works of charity. He argues that hibakusha

had a great need for nurturance and affection, and yet what attention they received was tainted by the suspicion that it was extended because they were survivors of the bomb, not because of who they were as individuals.

6. Lifton notes that hibakusha were furious over President Truman's continual reiteration that he had "no regrets" about ordering the dropping of the bomb. The Japanese have a strong "cultural stress upon reconciliation between contending groups through some form of apology which demonstrates concern for those one has injured, makes retaliation unnecessary, and permits re-establishment of harmony" (*Death in Life*, 334). McMillan's apology was restorative because it was imbued with her deeply felt sorrow and horror and rooted in a respectful understanding of Japanese cultural norms.

7. Doris Hartman, "A Tribute to Mary McMillan," *Japan Christian Quarterly* (Fall 1991): 224.

8. Mary McMillan, "The Cross-Bearing City: Hiroshima in the Movement for World Peace," *Japan Christian Quarterly* (January 1963): 12–13.

9. Barbara Reynolds, "Sailing into Test Waters," in *Reweaving the Web of Life,* ed. Pam McAllister (Philadelphia: New Society Press, 1982), 130.

10. Barbara Reynolds, *The Phoenix and the Dove* (Nagasaki: Nagasaki Appeal Committee, 1986), 3.

11. Lifton, *Death in Life,* 354.

12. Ibid., 343. Averill A. Liebow was a member of the Joint Commission for the Investigation of the Effects of the Atomic Bomb in Japan. His book, *Encounter with Disaster: A Medical Diary of Hiroshima, 1945* (New York: Norton, 1985) covers the crucial months from September 18 to December 6, 1945. Dr. Liebow exemplifies the attitude of the scientist: "once the deed was done, criminal or salutary, there was clearly a duty to perform, to measure not merely the power of a weapon soon to become outmoded or extinct, but the nature and extent of radiation injury in man" (*Encounter with Disaster,* 208).

13. William Schull, *Song among the Ruins* (Cambridge, Mass.: Harvard University Press, 1990), 127–28.

14. Reynolds, *The Phoenix and the Dove,* 12–13.

15. Captain Bigelow was a retired Word War II Naval Commander. The other crew members were William Reed Huntington, George Willoughby, and David Gale ("Friends in Action," *Newsweek,* February 10, 1958, 74–75).

16. Earle Reynolds, *Forbidden Voyage* (New York: McKay, 1961), 37. The book originated in articles that were serialized in the *Chugoku Shimbun.*

17. Reynolds, *The Phoenix and the Dove,* 17–18.

18. Reynolds, "Sailing into Test Waters," 133.

19. McMillan, "The Cross-Bearing City," 15.

20. Barbara Reynolds, "Recollections of Hiroshima and Future Plans," in "Goodbye to Hiroshima" (Hiroshima: Association to Express Appreciation to Barbara-San, June 1969, mimeographed), 10.

21. Dorothy Stroup and Mary McMillan, "Voyage to Nakhodka," mimeographed, 1961, 2–3.

22. Reynolds, *The Phoenix and the Dove,* 23.

23. Ibid., 26–27.

24. Miyoko and Hiro were chosen from a group of eighteen finalists by a panel of seven judges who represented various hibakusha and peace groups as well as professional and political leaders. There was some fear that ideological disagreements would preclude agreement on candidates, but there was almost unanimous agreement on these two young people. Candidates were asked to present a speech and were judged by the same standards used for English-language contests: sincerity, content, and delivery. Barbara commented that Miyoko had a "purity" that affected her listeners, a radiant sincerity about opposing nuclear weapons that would later be dulled by the adulation she received during their speaking tours.

25. Barbara brought a sensitivity to her role as cultural translator; unfortunately, there were other times when touring hibakusha encountered ignorance and retreated into fear. Some of these situations were caused by a poor choice of hibakusha for speaking trips; at other times there was insufficient care given to logistics in the host country, mistakes that arose from the language barrier, and a lack of attention to the emotional strain that could result from a constant repetition of their bomb stories.

26. Barbara talked about Hiro's grandmother with great affection and respect; her stories portrayed a formidable woman deeply rooted in Japanese culture and ethos, a woman whose strong sense of responsibility was passed on to her grandson.

27. Barbara Reynolds, interview by author, tape recording, Wilmington, Ohio, April 11, 1989.

28. Reynolds, *The Phoenix and the Dove,* 32.

29. Barbara Reynolds, "A Hibakusha Peace Pilgrimage," *Peace* 1, no. 3 (November 1963): 15–17. *Peace* was the quarterly publication of the American Pax Association, which in 1973 formed the organizational core for the U.S. branch of Pax Christi-USA. Pax Christi is a worldwide Catholic peace organization.

30. Barbara Reynolds, taped reflections sent to author, May 14, 1989.

31. Barbara Reynolds, "Peace Pilgrimage Report," mimeographed (Hiroshima: Peace Pilgrimage Committee, 1962), 1, 2.

32. Mizuhoko Kotani Asanuma, letter to author, January 24, 1990.

33. Reynolds, *The Phoenix and the Dove,* 44–45.

34. Reynolds, "Recollections of Hiroshima and Future Plans," 11–12.

35. Reynolds, *The Phoenix and the Dove,* 48.

36. Barbara Reynolds, "Voyage of Discovery," narrative of slide show photocopy (Hiroshima: World Friendship Center, 1984), 16.

37. Ibid., 17.

38. Miyao Ohara, "Editor's Note," in "Goodbye to Hiroshima," 27.

39. Tomin Harada, "Fifteen Years of the World Friendship Center," *Yu-Ai* (Hiroshima: World Friendship Center, 1980), 2. *Yu-Ai* ("Friendship") is the quarterly newsletter of the Friendship Center.

40. During the occupation Elizabeth Gray Vining, a Quaker educator and writer, was the tutor of Crown Prince (now Emperor) Akihito. Her

popular book, *Windows for the Crown Prince* (Philadelphia: Lippincott, 1952), is the narrative of that experience.

41. Barbara Reynolds, letter to Peace Resource Center, Wilmington College, July 27, 1989. A copy of the letter was sent to the author by Barbara Reynolds.

42. Dr. Tadatoshi Akiba, conversation with author, Boston, August 27, 1988. While a professor of mathematics at Tufts University, Dr. Akiba organized the Hibakusha Travel Grant Program, popularly known as the Akiba Project, which funded journalists for three-week research trips to Hiroshima and Nagasaki each August. The Akiba Project, which ran from 1979 to 1986, received generous support from Hiroshima media and the Hiroshima International Cultural Foundation and attracted excellent volunteer interpreters and organizers. I was a 1983 finalist, but did not receive one of the grants. My 1984 trip was self-funded, but I attribute part of its success to that initial association with the Akiba Project. Dr. Akiba continued to challenge and enhance my understanding of Hiroshima after my move to Boston in 1985. Dr. Akiba, a member of the Socialist Party, currently serves as Hiroshima's representative in the Diet.

43. Reynolds, *The Phoenix and the Dove,* 57.

44. Barbara Reynolds, "Hiroshima, City of Hope," unpaged photocopy (Hiroshima: World Friendship Center, 1965).

45. Lifton, *Death in Life,* 364.

46. Barbara Reynolds, "Hiroshima, Vietnam: Sisters in Sorrow," *Christian Century* 84 (May 10, 1967): 637–38.

47. There is a clear explanation of *on* in Ruth Benedict's classic work *The Chrysanthemum and the Sword: Patterns of Japanese Culture* (New York: New American Library, 1974).

48. I experienced both aspects of this: Admiring her voluntary poverty, knowing that her budget allowed few diversions, I occasionally sent Barbara money with the hopes that it would be used for modest recreation. Invariably, the funds would be passed on to others, so eventually I took to sending material goods: wool, books, stationery, stamps, etc. Barbara honestly felt that she did not need the many gifts and honors she received and passed material goods on in a spirit of providential trust. Sharing and understanding that philosophy, I had little difficulty accepting her decision to give my gifts away. However, I could readily understand the offense and anger felt by Japanese people, with different societal attitudes concerning gifts and obligations. In 1989, Barbara subsidized my air fare to Wilmington from funds that had been sent her by a peace group in Sendai, Japan; she reasoned that our work was an expression of "Hiroshima peace work" and thus would be an appropriate use of their generous gift.

49. Barbara Reynolds, "Regaining Our Humanity," in Ground Zero Center for Non-Violent Action, *No Rest for "Da Fence": Trident Trials 1980* (Poulsbo, Wash.: Ground Zero Center, 1980), 40–41.

50. Barbara Reynolds, interview by author, tape recording, Wilmington, Ohio, April 13, 1989.

51. Sadako Sasaki was exposed to the bomb when she was two years old; although seemingly unhurt, the significant radiation exposure she re-

ceived led to her death from leukemia a decade later. The story of Sadako (whom some have called "the Anne Frank of Hiroshima") has become symbolic of the suffering of children in war. One of the most popular children's books about Hiroshima is Eleanor Coerr's *Sadako and the Thousand Paper Cranes* (New York: Avon, 1971). The crane is a symbol of longevity and good fortune, and Japanese legend holds that the folding of one thousand paper cranes will guarantee one's wish will come true. Sadako was folding paper cranes in her final illness, but died before she completed them. Her classmates folded the rest and went on to raise funds for a statue in her honor. One of the most impressive monuments in the Peace Park, it is always festooned with leis of paper cranes.

52. Kawamoto's story is among those told in the beautiful photographs (Eikoh Hosoe) and evocative text (Betty Jean Lifton) of *A Place Called Hiroshima* (New York: Kodansha, 1985). This is a haunting, nonintrusive book about the invisible wounds of Hiroshima. Kawamoto was also portrayed in *Children of the Ashes: The Story of a Rebirth,* by Austrian writer Robert Jungk (New York: Harcourt, Brace, 1961).

53. Barbara Reynolds, interview by author, tape recording, Wilmington, Ohio, April 10, 1989.

Chapter 4 – The Betrayal of Loyalty: American Hibakusha

1. Amy Iwasaki Mass, "Psychological Effects of the Camps on Japanese Americans," in Roger Daniels, Sandra C. Taylor, and Harry H. L. Kitano. eds., *Japanese Americans: From Relocation to Redress,* rev. ed. (Seattle: University of Washington Press, 1991), 160.

2. Ibid., 161.

3. David L. Swain, in a note to the author (October 30, 1994), indicated that "peasant rebellions, urban riots, rice (price) riots, and labor struggles go back several hundred years in Japan....What is typical is reticence to push one's *individual* rights (vs. group rights)."

4. Takeo Doi, *The Anatomy of Dependence,* trans. John Bester (New York: Kodansha, 1981), 15.

5. John Bester, foreword to *The Anatomy of Dependence,* 7–9.

6. Rinjiro Sodei, "Were We the Enemy?" unpublished manuscript of English translation, 194. I am indebted to Professor Sodei for the opportunity to have read and critiqued the English translation of his book about American hibakusha. It was originally published in Japan in 1982. Sodei's book is at times marred by acerbic or overly sentimental prose, although it is difficult to know if this is due to the English translation, and while this can be irritating to an American reader it is valuable to read a Japanese perspective about the bomb.

7. "California: The Secret Sufferers," *Newsweek,* April 10, 1972, 26.

8. Joy Zimmerman, "Hiroshima Revisited," *Pacific Sun,* week of August 7–13, 1987, 3. Dorothy Stroup is the author of *In the Autumn Wind* (New York: Scribner's, 1985). Stroup taught at Hiroshima Jogakuin Women's College in the early 1960s and although what she learned about the bomb informed her short fiction, it was not until an extensive 1979

research trip to Hiroshima that she "had the eerie feeling of being chosen. It seemed to me that there was no one else at that moment who knew the things I knew, and who could write about them in English to tell the human story of this atomic experience." She has done this admirably well through the life of her protagonist, a Japanese housewife. A resident of Berkeley, where she has taught for many years, Stroup is an active member of Friends of Hibakusha, a group that supports the activities of American hibakusha.

9. Sodei, "Were We the Enemy?" 194.

10. Harry H. L. Kitano, "The Effects of Evacuation," in Daniels et al., *Japanese Americans: From Relocation to Redress,* 156–57.

11. Teresa Watanabe, "Japan Helps U.S. Victims of A-Bomb," *San Jose (California) Mercury News,* July 31, 1988, section A, 28.

12. It is uncertain if publicity about secret radiation tests conducted during the 1950s will have an impact on the organizing efforts of American hibakusha.

13. The figure of 3,200 is cited by Peter Wyden in *Day One* (New York: Simon and Schuster, 1984), 274.

14. Kanji Kuramoto, "Voices of the Survivors," *The Paper Crane* 6, no. 1 (Winter 1991): 3. *The Paper Crane* is a publication of the Friends of Hibakusha. "Voices of the Survivors" included excerpts from the Hibakusha History Project.

15. Jane Iwashika, "Remembering," in *The Paper Crane* 1, no. 1 (Spring 1983): 4.

16. Sodei, "Were We the Enemy?" 24–25.

17. Mary Jo McConahay, "First Person Nuclear," in *The Paper Crane* 1, no. 1 (Spring 1983): 2. This was reprinted (in part) from *San Francisco Magazine.*

18. Watanabe, "Japan Helps," 28.

19. McConahay, "First Person Nuclear," 2.

20. Dorothy Stroup, "The Role of the Japanese American Press in its Community." M.A. diss., University of California at Berkeley, 1960.

21. Mass, "Psychological Effects," 159.

22. Sodei, "Were We the Enemy?" 56.

23. Dan Ouellette and Evantheia Schibsted, "Unclaimed Casualties," *San Francisco Examiner,* August 4, 1991, *Image* magazine, 24.

24. Ibid.

25. Dorothy Stroup, "Anytime, Anywhere: Memories of Kuniko," *The Paper Crane* (Summer 1986): 1.

26. *The Paper Crane* (Fall 1988): 1.

27. Ouellette and Schibsted, "Unclaimed Casualties," 24.

28. "Voices of Survivors," *The Paper Crane,* 4.

29. Iwashika, "Remembering."

30. Sodei, "Were We the Enemy?" 229.

31. Ronald Takaki, *Strangers from a Distant Shore: A History of Asian Americans* (New York: Penguin, 1990), 46.

32. *Harvard Encyclopedia of American Ethnic Groups,* s.v. "Japanese."

33. Medical and financial aid for hibakusha is a highly political issue. In 1975, Hiroshima physicians, peace activists, and city officials extended a warm welcome to residents of Bikini Atoll who had suffered from radiation exposure during American hydrogen bomb testing. They were assured that "although the U.S. Medical Law placed obstacles in the way of sending doctors directly, they would examine and treat any islanders who could come to Hiroshima" (*The Meaning of Survival: Hiroshima's 36 Year Commitment to Peace* [Hiroshima: Chugoku Shimbun, 1983], 242).

34. Sodei, "Were We the Enemy?" 181–82.

35. *Harvard Encyclopedia,* 563–64.

36. Sodei, "Were We the Enemy?" 160–61.

37. The Committee for the Compilation of Materials on Damage Caused by the Atomic Bombs in Hiroshima and Nagasaki, *Hiroshima and Nagasaki: The Physical, Medical and Social Effects of the Atomic Bombings,* trans. Eisei Ishikawa and David L. Swain (New York: Basic Books, 1981), 465.

38. Ibid.

39. Lee Gi-Sang, "The Unknown Victims," in *Hibakusha: Survivors of Hiroshima and Nagasaki* (Tokyo: Kosei Publishing Company, 1986), 120.

40. Ibid., 134.

41. David L. Swain, letter to author, February 28, 1994.

42. "Hiroshima: Living in the Nuclear Age" (Hiroshima: Hiroshima Institute of Peace Education, 1980), 71.

43. The Hiroshima A-Bomb Teachers' Association has raised some funds to offset transportation costs for American hibakusha, but this has helped only a limited number of people, as have fundraising efforts by Friends of Hibakusha. In a letter to the author dated February 28, 1994, David L. Swain pointed out that Japanese Christian groups took initiatives to bring Korean hibakusha to Japan, their help includes assistance to victims' families who are deprived of breadwinners' earnings while they are away.

44. *Meaning of Survival,* 235.

45. Ouellette and Schibsted, "Unclaimed Casualties," 24.

46. Sodei, "Were We the Enemy?" 279–80.

47. Ouellette and Schibsted, "Unclaimed Casualties," 23.

48. Sodei, "Were We the Enemy?" 274.

49. *Harvard Encyclopedia,* s.v. "Japanese."

50. Sodei, "Were We the Enemy?" 225–26.

51. Stroup, "In the Shadow of Hiroshima," 12.

Chapter 5 – The Mystic of Nagasaki: Takashi Nagai, M.D.

1. The Committee for the Compilation of Materials on Damage Caused by the Atomic Bombs in Hiroshima and Nagasaki, *Hiroshima and Nagasaki: The Physical, Medical, and Social Effects of the Atomic Bombings,* trans. Eisei Ishikawa and David L. Swain (New York: Basic Books, 1981), 382.

2. Ibid., 344.

3. Ibid., 381.

4. Robert Lifton, *Death in Life: Survivors of Hiroshima* (New York: Random House, 1967), 312–13.

5. Ibid., 307.

6. Sadao Kamata and Stephen Salaff, "The Atomic Bomb and the Citizens of Nagasaki," in *The Other Japan: Postwar Realities,* ed. E. Patricia Tsurumi (Armonk, N.Y.: M. E. Sharpe, 1988), 65.

7. Hugh V. Clarke, a POW in Nagasaki, tells of his imprisonment and his A-bomb experience in his memoir *Last Stop Nagasaki!* (London: George Allen & Unwin, 1984).

8. Kamata and Salaff, "Citizens of Nagasaki," 61.

9. "Japan: Tale of Two Cities," *Time,* May 18, 1962, 28.

10. Takashi Nagai, *The Bells of Nagasaki,* trans. William Johnston (New York: Kodansha, 1984), 109.

11. Father Johnston is well-known as a writer, translator, and specialist on the dialogue between Zen Buddhism and Christianity. He is a professor at Tokyo's Sofia University. Three of Dr. Nagai's eleven books have been translated into English, but the only one currently in print is Father Johnston's translation of *The Bells of Nagasaki. We of Nagasaki* and *Living under the Atomic Cloud* are both out of print.

12. Pius DeVoti, S.X., telephone conversation with author, May 11, 1994. Father DeVoti, an Italian Xaverian, spent fifteen years as a missionary in Japan and currently serves the Japanese Apostolate in the archdiocese of Boston.

13. Nagai, *Bells of Nagasaki,* 109.

14. *New Catholic Encyclopedia,* s.v. "Japan, Martyrs of."

15. Everett F. Briggs, *New Dawn in Japan* (New York: Longmans, Green & Co., 1948), 69.

16. *New Catholic Encyclopedia,* s.v. "Japan, Martyrs of."

17. Edward Fischer, *Japan Journey: The Columban Fathers in Nippon* (New York: Crossroad, 1984), 29.

18. The 26 martyrs, whose feast day is celebrated on February 3, were beatified in 1627 and canonized in 1862. In 1867 Pope Pius IV beatified 205 Japanese Christians who died between 1617 and 1632. There were an estimated 35,000 martyrs during the persecution, but as Jesuit father J. Laures noted, "It is simply impossible to procure even approximately accurate statistics on the positively endless number of those who were robbed of their possessions, driven out of house and home, thrown into prison, tortured in all conceivable manners to make them apostatize, or exiled from their country for the sake of Christ" (*New Catholic Encyclopedia,* s.v. "Japan, Martyrs of").

19. Kamata and Salaff, "Citizens of Nagasaki," 64.

20. Euan Cameron, "For Whom the Bell Tolls," *The Tablet,* July 29, 1989, 862.

21. Nagasaki's current mayor, Hitoshi Motoshima, is a descendent of these Hidden Christians. He notes the irony that it was Burakumin, traditional outcasts, who "were driven to undesirable, barren lands and charged with the task of spying on Christians. Thus have minorities been

prevented from making common cause" (Norma Field, *In the Realm of a Dying Emperor* [New York: Pantheon, 1991], 240).

22. William J. Schull, *Song among the Ruins* (Cambridge, Mass.: Harvard University Press, 1990), 196.

23. Ibid.

24. Kamata and Salaff, "Citizens of Nagasaki," 64.

25. William D. Bray, "The Hidden Christians of Ikutsuki Island," *Japan Christian Quarterly* (April 1960): 82.

26. Paul Glynn, *A Song for Nagasaki* (Grand Rapids, Mich.: Eerdmans, 1990), 101–2.

27. Nagai, *Bells of Nagasaki*, 108.

28. Ibid., 106–7.

29. Ibid., 118.

30. Glynn, *Song for Nagasaki*, 116–17.

31. Ibid., 127–28.

32. Ibid., 173.

33. Nagai, *Bells of Nagasaki*, 12.

34. Ibid., 33.

35. Ibid., 37.

36. Takashi Nagai, *We of Nagasaki: The Story of Survivors in an Atomic Wasteland*, trans. Ichiro Shirato and Herbert B. L. Silverman (New York: Duell, Sloan and Pearce, 1958), 181.

37. Ibid., 182–83.

38. Nagai, *Bells of Nagasaki*, 83.

39. Ibid., 80.

40. Ibid.

41. Ibid., 60.

42. Nagai, *Bells of Nagasaki*, 108.

43. Glynn, *Song for Nagasaki*, 238–39.

44. David L. Swain, review of *The Bells of Nagasaki*, by Takashi Nagai, *Japan Christian Quarterly* (Summer 1985): 182.

45. Nagai, *We of Nagasaki*, 189.

46. Ibid., 166.

47. Ibid., 172–73.

48. Ibid., 171–72.

49. Tatsuichiro Akizuki, *Nagasaki 1945*, trans. Keiichi Nagata (London: Quartet Books, 1981), 120.

50. David L. Swain, "Portrait of a Peacemaker (2) — Akizuki Tatsuichiro," *Japan Christian Quarterly* (Winter 1985): 49.

51. Ibid., 50.

52. Ibid., 49.

53. Kamata and Salaff, "Citizens of Nagasaki," 66.

54. William Johnston, S.J., note to author, June 8, 1994.

55. Nagai, *Bells of Nagasaki*, 106.

56. Nagai, Ibid., 109.

57. Glynn, *Song for Nagasaki*, 109.

Chapter 6 –In the Company of Hibakusha

1. Andre Ryerson, "The Cult of Hiroshima," *Commentary* 38 (October 1985): 36–40.

2. Ibid., 40.

3. Rita M. Barnes, "Letter to the Editor," *Boston Herald,* August 25, 1985.

4. Peter Jennings, "Many Thanks for a Job Well Done," in *Harper's,* October 1985, 20. The excerpt was taken from Jennings's final remarks on the ABC news broadcast from Hiroshima on August 5, 1985.

5. Don March, "In War, Evil Drives Out Good," *Charlestown (W. Va.) Gazette,* August 4, 1984.

6. Eduardo Cohen, "Nagasaki Remembered," *Boston Globe,* August 6, 1989.

7. Edita Morris, *The Flowers of Hiroshima* (New York: Pocket Books, 1963), 184–85.

Index

$\mathcal{CB}$

143